A *Woman's* Passionate Pursuit of God

CREATING A POSITIVE & PURPOSEFUL LIFE

KAROL LADD

HARVEST HOUSE PUBLISHERS

EUGENE, OREGON

Cover by Koechel Peterson & Associates, Inc., Minneapolis, Minnesota

Cover photo © Thomas Northcutt / Photodisc / Thinkstock

Backcover author photo by Shooting Starr Photography by Cindi Starr, www.shootingstarrphotos.com

A WOMAN'S PASSIONATE PURSUIT OF GOD
Copyright © 2011 by Karol Ladd
Published by Harvest House Publishers
Eugene, Oregon 97402
www.harvesthousepublishers.com

Library of Congress Cataloging-in-Publication Data

Ladd, Karol.
A woman's passionate pursuit of God / Karol Ladd.
p. cm.
Includes bibliographical references.
ISBN 978-0-7369-2964-6 (pbk.)
1. Christian women—Religious life. 2. Christian life—Biblical teaching. 3. Bible. N.T. Philippians—Criticism, interpretation, etc. I. Title.
BV4527.L2533 2011
248.8'43—dc22

2010015987

Printed in the United States of America

11 12 13 14 15 16 17 18 / VP-NI / 10 9 8 7 6 5 4 3 2

*This book is dedicated to every woman who has
ever experienced even an inkling of a desire to
passionately pursue Christ. May your love for Him
grow deeper still as a result of reading this book.*

Thank you to all my wonderful friends at Harvest House Publishers. Bob, LaRae, Shane, Peggy, and everyone who has played a part in this book and video project, it is a true blessing and joy to work with you. Thank you for your commitment to excellence and the truth of God's Word. Thank you also to all the women who allowed me to share their stories and passion for God in order to inspire others on their journeys.

Contents

*C*hasing Happiness and Finding Joy

*For I want you to understand what really matters, so that
you may live pure and blameless lives until Christ returns.*
—PHILIPPIANS 1:10

*To seek God is to desire happiness; to
find him is that happiness.*
—AUGUSTINE

Spring in Dallas just doesn't make sense to me. On any given day, we may have a freeze warning at nightfall and 80 degree temperatures by the very next afternoon. It's crazy! They say if you don't like the weather in Texas, just stay around for a couple of hours, and it'll change.

On a recent March morning, I stepped outside to get the newspaper and was hit with a blizzard. Well, it may not have been that extreme, but it was one of those take-your-breath-away cold fronts that felt like a blizzard to this thin-blooded Southern girl. By mid afternoon of that very same day, I was sitting in the garden reading and enjoying some good ole Texas sunshine.

Personally, I love to be outside, and I love to read, so when I can find the time to enjoy both, it is a happy afternoon. On this particular spring day, my personal reading agenda was the book of Philippians in the New Testament of the Bible. Written by the apostle Paul while he was a prisoner in Rome, one could easily assume Philippians would be a real downer of a book. On the contrary, it is quite a delightful and uplifting read. In fact, the theme of joy—from this unlikely author—sort of oozes through the pages.

As I relaxed and tried to picture how Paul could possibly write such a positive message from a prison cell, I glanced up to see a white butterfly dancing around our garden. I watched with amusement this fluttering creature touch a flower here, flit off to another flower there, dart to several others, and then fly back to where it had begun. It never stayed in one place for more than a few seconds as if it were pursuing something it would never find. Just as quickly as it appeared in my garden, it was off to the next field of flowers.

Observing the illusive dance of the white butterfly made me think about how illusive life's pleasures can be. Just like this flitting creature, I realized how easy it is for me to flit, flutter, and fly from one activity or person to another, trying to find sweet nectar to satisfy my longings for significance and joy. I'm guessing you have felt those same feelings a time or two as well. The pursuit of happiness is common to us all. The question is: Where does the chase stop, or does it stop? Are we fooling ourselves into thinking that there is something out there that will enrich our beings and fill the hunger of our souls?

The Happiness Hunt

Hunting for happiness can often tease us. Consider the money, time, and energy we expend during our lives chasing the intriguing "if onlys" of life. You know what I mean; if only…then I will be happy.

- If only I could date a wonderful guy
- If only I could go to the right college
- If only I could find the best job

- If only I could marry the perfect man
- If only I had married that other man
- If only I could have well-behaved kids
- If only my kids could make the cheerleader squad, sports team, or special interest club
- If only I had time to relax, money to spend, a house that is clean, or a life that is simple

Phew! We can wear ourselves out just thinking about all the possible opportunities to experience happiness, and I didn't even mention the physical perfections we chase. If only I had

- pretty hair
- thinner thighs
- toned arms
- fewer wrinkles
- a smaller tummy
- a different nose

Then I would be happy! Right?

Sounds like white butterflies flitting around from one flower to another! Oh, I'm not saying these things won't make us happy. They very well may generate happy feelings for a while, but typically once we have experienced an "if only," it's on to the pursuit of the next hopeful dream. The point is feelings of happiness come and go. Vance Havner put it this way, "The world's happiness should be spelled 'happen-ness' because it depends on what happens."[1] We may be happy because we just got a raise, or someone is nice to us, or the kitchen is finally redecorated, but then the hunt is on for the next happy happening. The pursuit of happiness simply takes us from one sweet flower to the next.

What Really Matters

The irony of my butterfly encounter on that spring day in Dallas is that I was sitting there reading a book that highlighted enduring qualities that transcended shifting circumstances and fleeting feelings. Paul (yes, from his prison cell) described a resilient joy, a consistent contentment, and a peace that passes all understanding in his letter to the Philippians. Unlike the flitting butterfly, Paul taught the early Christians how to experience a true satisfaction of the soul.

Does God call us to pursue happiness or to pursue Him and His purposes in our life? In the book of Philippians, Paul paints a fresh perspective on life for us. He challenges us to live and think differently than the world around us. If this man in prison can write about being "full of joy," then I think he has something to teach us about a type of meaningful fulfillment and deeper delight beyond circumstances or people.

Ultimately Paul encourages us to chase what is eternally satisfying, a pursuit that will not disappoint. I'm inviting you to join me on an exhilarating journey as we walk together through Paul's joy-filled letter to the Philippians. You will never look at the challenges in your life the same way again. I believe you will discover a type of soul satisfaction that brings lasting fulfillment.

A Woman's Passionate Pursuit of God is about experiencing a joy that won't go away. It's about finding a true contentment and an eternal purpose for your life as we discover the powerful truths Paul presented in his letter to the followers of Christ at Philippi. There are a variety of ways you can take in the truths of this book. You can use this book for your own personal reading, a neighborhood book club, or a large group Bible study. At the end of each chapter, you will find a section called "Personal Pursuit." Read it to learn ways to apply what you have learned from each chapter to your life right now. At the end of the book, you will find a study guide with discussion questions to use in Bible study or book groups.

It is with great joy that I offer this book to you because the powerful message of Philippians has gripped my life personally. Although I'm known as the "Positive Lady," I must be honest with you, I'm not so sure how positive I would be if it were not for the transforming work God has done in my life. I don't know if you are generally a negative person or if you lean toward the positive, but I do know that the truths presented in Philippians can bring joy, inspiration, and strength to help you in whatever you are facing in life.

A Woman's Passionate Pursuit of God leads you on a life-changing adventure toward a more intimate encounter with the Lover of your soul. Yet the ultimate pursuit is not our pursuit of Him, but rather His pursuit of us. God comes after us with a redeeming love and a hope-filled grace. My prayer is that this book will strengthen your heart as you recognize you are dearly loved by Him. May you experience a lasting joy and a peaceful satisfaction, which only comes from a deep and abiding relationship with Him.

> Surely your goodness and
>   unfailing love will pursue me
>   all the days of my life,
> and I will live in the house of the Lord
>   forever.[2]
> —David

CHAPTER ONE

Beautiful Hope from Ugly Beginnings

I will praise the LORD at all times.
I will constantly speak his praises.
I will boast only in the LORD;
let all who are helpless take heart.

—PSALM 34:1-2 NLT

There are no lessons so useful as those
learned in the school of affliction.

—J.D. RYLE

Bad starts don't always determine how you finish. I've had a few rough starts in my life, and I'm sure you have too. Take, for instance, the one and only marathon I ran back in my college days as a student at Baylor University. That's 26.2 miles for those of you who are not necessarily running enthusiasts. When I lined up at the starting line of this momentous marathon race, I somehow didn't realize thousands of other people would be joining me. I guess I assumed only a few people on this earth would choose to run in a 26.2 mile race. Well, let me tell you there were so many people that I couldn't even see the flags marking the starting line. I began the race way, way, way back in the pack, and it took what seemed like an hour just to get beyond those first flags. Of course, I couldn't even think about stopping to tie my shoe or taking a look behind me. One false move and I would have been trampled by thousands of Nikes.

Eventually the crowd began to thin out, and I worked into a pretty confident stride until I began to face new challenges—like blisters in places I never imagined a person could have blisters and my socks feeling like sandbags around my feet. Four hours and thirty-two minutes later, I crossed the finish line with a smile of victory and a hearty sense of accomplishment (and relief). I made it! I can't begin to describe the feeling of excitement I experienced knowing I set a goal and achieved it. The point is I didn't have such a glorious start to the race, but through persistence and perseverance, there was a grand and sweet outcome. At dinner that night, we celebrated my triumph with family and friends, and, of course, I fell asleep in the middle of my mashed potatoes.

No doubt it is easy for any of us to become discouraged when we have rough spots in our lives, especially if they happen at the beginning of our journey. Maybe your marriage started on a negative note, your career got off on the wrong path, or your childhood years were a disaster. It could be that you simply had a bad start to your day and felt defeated even before you got out the door. The good news is no matter how you start your journey, the beginning doesn't necessarily determine the outcome. There are tremendous possibilities up ahead. God is a God of hope, and He can bring redemption to even the worst situations.

Take the humble beginnings of the Philippian church for example. You would think this church had a stellar start when you sense the joy shining brightly from the pages of the book of Philippians. Oddly, it wasn't so good for Paul and Silas. In fact, it was downright awful! Yet God used the challenges of Paul and Silas and the Philippians to birth a strong and vibrant church. As we take a look at Paul's situation and the story of the first converts in Philippi, we not only see a picture of hope, but we can also gain insight into wise and prudent ways to react when our life is not going as we planned.

A Major Mess in the Middle of God's Will

When you follow God's leading in your life, don't you tend to think everything should go smoothly? Personally, I often assume that when I am following God, He will reward me with nice pleasant circumstances in my life, not bumpy roads and potholes. Yet life doesn't always play out like a neat little math equation: Obedience + Good Works = Easy Life. Paul and Silas were doing the right things right. They sought God's direction and guidance as they set out on their missionary journey. We read in Acts 16 that Paul and his team steered clear of certain locations because God's Spirit told them not to go there. Just when they were wondering about where they should go, Paul had a dream about a man in Macedonia who was pleading, "Come over to Macedonia and help us!" Paul, Silas, Luke, and the rest of the group immediately packed up and left for Macedonia. Without a doubt, they were sincerely following God's instructions.

When they arrived on the shores of Macedonia, Paul's team traveled inland to a major city called Philippi. Down by the river, they found several women who had come together to pray. This most likely meant there were not enough Jewish men in the city to start a synagogue. Lydia, a seller of expensive purple cloth, listened to Paul's message, and God opened her heart to the gospel. She believed and was baptized along with those in her household. Isn't it beautiful to note that back in a day when women had little social status, God allowed the first recorded convert in Europe to be a woman? We see throughout the New Testament that God used women to play an important part in the growth of the early church. Lydia opened her home to Paul and Silas in a grateful gesture of hospitality, and all seemed to be going well for the missionaries.

It's amazing to me how quickly circumstances can change. Paul and his friends were on their way to the place of prayer when they met up with a demon-possessed slave girl. She was a fortune-teller who brought in quite a bit of money for her masters. Whether or not she could really tell the future is doubtful. Many theologians believe that demons cannot see the future, but we do know they can see the spirit realm and are deceptive in nature, and they obviously gave this girl some sort of insight.

She followed Paul's group, shouting, "These men are servants of the Most High God, and they have come to tell you how to be saved." This went on day after day. Now you may be tempted to think that the girl's proclamation wasn't so bad because she was endorsing Paul and his message, but Paul didn't need an endorsement from demons. Think about a political candidate who gets an endorsement from a constituency group who has a very different set of values. He may not want a pat on the back from that particular group. Paul was actually becoming exasperated by the slave girl's loud announcements, so he did what seemed kind and good. He healed her by casting out the demon.

This is where the situation started to go downhill. The masters of the slave girl could no longer make a profit off of her, and they were fighting mad! They grabbed Paul and Silas, dragged them before the authorities at the marketplace, and accused them of causing all sorts of disturbances. A mob quickly formed, and the officials ordered Paul and Silas to be beaten. This was no light punishment. They were severely beaten and cast into the inner prison, and their legs were put into stocks. If I were Paul or Silas, I would be thinking, *What just happened? How did we go from talking about Jesus to getting beaten up and thrown in the dungeon? Didn't God call us to this place? Weren't we only doing what was right? Now what?*

Have you ever thought you were following God's guidance or leading and found yourself in a real mess of a situation? It can tend to make you want to doubt God and question His work in your life. *Did I really follow God's direction? Does He really care about my situation? Why would God allow this to happen to me if I am following His will?* The questions are valid, but we will soon see that God often allows the difficulties in our lives for a greater purpose. He will not leave us in the midst of our troubles. The important thing is to learn to react to our situations and challenges with faith and not fear.

Faith Reaction

If I were unfairly beaten and thrown in the deepest, darkest prison with my feet in stocks, I'm not sure how well I would react. I don't even react well when my husband asks me what's for dinner. And woe be it to him if he dares to ask me when is the next time I plan to use the vacuum! Oh, and I'm pretty certain if I were locked up for doing something good, I would cry and groan and whine, so everyone would know about my pitiful situation. I may even panic and scream. Of course, I wish I could tell you I would react with dignity and hope in every difficult and desperate situation, but that hasn't exactly been my consistent pattern. What about you?

So how did Paul and Silas react? They prayed and praised God! Yes, you read that right. They sat there in their stocks, praying and praising God. In fact, the Bible tells us the other prisoners listened intently. Now, the observant prisoners probably didn't have a whole lot of other things going on in the deepest darkest dungeon, but I can imagine they were honestly shocked by the way Paul and Silas acted. This was certainly a strange response to cruel torture and unfair punishment. I'm sure Paul and Silas had the guards' *and* the other prisoners' attention.

Now here is an important lesson for each of us to learn—our reaction to any situation can make an impact on the outcome. A silly story I recently came across illustrates my point. Mrs. Monroe is the mother of eight precious children. Upon returning from the grocery store one day, Mrs. Monroe was delighted to see five of her children playing nicely in a circle on the living room floor. After putting away all the groceries, she decided to peak into the circle to see what was holding the kids' attention in such a gentle way. It was then that she realized this was not the sweet situation she imagined because she saw that each child was holding a cute, soft baby skunk!

Of course, Mrs. Monroe reacted like any self-respecting mother would. She screamed at the top of her lungs, "Run, children, run!" The kids were so startled by their mother's scream that they immediately took to flight, but not without grabbing their precious little treasured skunks and squeezing them tightly as they ran! Well, I think we could safely say that Mrs. Monroe's reaction had a somewhat stinky effect on the outcome.[1]

We may not be able to choose our circumstances, but we can certainly choose our response to them. As we saw with Mrs. Monroe, the way we choose to respond can have a positive or a negative effect on what happens next. Paul and Silas had a choice when it came to the way they responded to their surprising and difficult circumstances. They could have chosen to shout out in rage about all the unlawful actions that had happened to them that day, and the guards would have probably responded by beating them into silence. But Paul and Silas chose to react in faith. They deliberately did the opposite of what comes naturally. Think about it! They probably didn't feel like praying and praising God, but they chose to do it anyway. They chose a faith reaction in the midst of a fearful situation.

I can imagine they began praising God for His sovereignty and power. They probably praised God because He could and would use this situation for His glory. I'm guessing they thanked God for the privilege of sharing in Christ's sufferings. They may have prayed for the jailers and other prisoners. Maybe they prayed that God would heal and help them get through this situation in faith. Whatever they prayed, we know it had an impact on the people around them.

Paul's example serves as an inspiration to us all to do more praying and less whining. When dealing with the little simple snags to our day—much less the big life-changing challenges—I would venture to say most of us struggle to react in faith. Our reaction is a choice. Often we fall into a comfortable habit of getting upset or worrying in response to a situation. Let's determine to choose faith over fear and gratitude over grumbling. I'm reminded of Paul's letter to the Corinthian church where we see his faith in God shining brightly even in the midst of extremely challenging situations. Here's what he said, "We have this treasure in jars of clay to show that this all-surpassing power is from God and not from us. We are hard pressed on every side, but not crushed; perplexed, but not in despair; persecuted, but not abandoned; struck down, but not destroyed."[2]

How did Paul and Silas do it? They prayerfully turned to God immediately in the midst of their despairing circumstances. They praised God even in the pit. They didn't ignore or gloss over the pain they were going through, but they chose to look at it in a different way. They chose to look up, and they realized their power to get through the difficulties came from God and not from themselves. We too can learn to turn our eyes upward and have a different response than the rest of the world when it comes to the challenges in our life. We are jars of clay with a great and mighty God who is able to bring beauty out of any situation. He will give us the strength we need to endure and persevere through the not-so-perfect places in our lives.

Dramatic Rescue

God answered Paul and Silas' prayers! At midnight there was a great earthquake, and the prison was shaken to its foundation. All the doors flew open, and the chains on every prisoner fell off. Every prisoner? I understand why God would free Paul and Silas, but did He really mean to free all the prisoners? And what do you think those prisoners did? Well, if I were one of those prisoners, I would have run! But now here's the peculiar thing, none of them ran. Not one! Hmmm, I have to scratch my head and wonder why they didn't flee.

Could it be that they looked at Paul and Silas, and after watching them pray and praise God, they decided they wanted to know more about their God? Maybe they saw the dramatic answer to their prayers and thought, *Man, I'm sticking with these guys. Their God is God!* Whatever was going through their minds, I do think it is incredible that all the prisoners stayed. It's a humble reminder that others are watching us. People who do not know Christ are watching how we respond to difficult situations. Do we show them a different response than those who do not know Christ? Do others see the way we react in faith—and not fear—and say, "I want to know more about their God"? I dare say, if we truly live like people who believe in Christ by reacting to circumstances with hearts of faith, then many would be drawn to Him.

My friend Mary is a good example of someone whose godly response to difficulties has made an impact on others. You see, Mary received the type of phone call no wife wants to receive. Her dearly beloved husband of more than 15 years had been tragically killed in a biking accident. Mary and her three children grieved and cried through the painful loss of their godly husband and father. Yet through the pain, Mary's faith and hope remained constant. She had a deep sense God was with her, holding her and her children in the midst of her sorrow. Her husband's coworkers knew of his faith and were amazed and fascinated to observe the faith of his widow. Mary began reaching out to those in her husband's company who didn't know or want to believe in God. She gave one coworker a Bible with his name engraved on it (so he couldn't regift it), and she corresponded with him and others to help them on their journey of faith.

Her faith-filled response to her husband's death made an impact on every life that was touched by the tragedy. Her response doesn't change the fact that he is gone, but it does change the way she works through her grief and the impact it has on others. She has discovered a sense of joy by bringing the truth and comfort of the gospel to thirsty souls. Of course, she grieves and cries, but she also knows an inner peace and strength that only comes from turning her hurt and her pain over to the God who loves her. She is seeing God show up in ways she couldn't ever imagine. Mary says she has learned not to live in fear and worry about what lies ahead, but to prayerfully give her concerns to God day by day. Other people see her faith in action and are drawn to her Savior. Keep shining, Mary! Shine on![3]

The Ultimate Question

God turns despair into hope. He has done so in Mary's life, and we can see it in Paul and Silas' lives as well. There they were in the deepest darkest dungeon in what seemed like hopeless circumstances, but now the tables have turned. Paul and Silas are set free, and the jailer is in despair. When the jailer dusted off the debris from the earthquake, he saw the open prison doors and assumed the prisoners had all run free. Typically jailers were tortured with the same punishment their prisoners were to receive if their prisoners escaped. The jailer thought his only hope was to kill himself.

Yet God always provides true hope! Paul quickly called out to the jailer and reassured him that all of the prisoners were present. The jailer fell on his knees before Paul and Silas and asked the most important question anyone on this earth could ask: What must I do to be saved? In a dramatic switch of circumstances, the jailer asks the prisoners how to be set free. Whether he realized it or not, the jailer asked the question we must all ask at some point in our life: How can I be free from the guilt of my own wrongdoing? When the jailer asked the ultimate question, Paul and Silas didn't even hesitate with their answer. They didn't offer several ways to be saved and let the jailer choose what works for him. No, they were quite clear and unmistakably direct with their response. The final answer to the jailer's ultimate question was (and still is), "Believe in the Lord Jesus and you will be saved."

The decision was clear, and the jailer believed in Christ. But that's not the end of the story. The jailer believed, and his life was transformed. In Acts 16 we read that Paul and Silas shared the truth about Jesus Christ with the jailer and all who lived in his household. The jailer then washed Paul and Silas' wounds. Imagine that! The one who was on the side of those who beat the prisoners is now the one caring for their wounds and bandaging them up. The Bible says the jailer was baptized along with everyone in his house. The family then invited Paul and Silas into their home, fed them, and rejoiced because they all believed in God.

Faith in Christ made a difference in his life. This was not the same jailer who threw the battered and beaten missionaries into the center of the prison and placed them in stocks. He had been transformed into a kind and joyful man, no longer in despair. When a person places their faith in Christ, they are no longer the same. Paul wrote to the Corinthian church, "Therefore, if anyone is in Christ, he is a new creation; the old has gone, the new has come!"[4] When we follow Christ, God begins a new work in us. His Spirit dwells within us and gives us the power and strength to react differently than the rest of the world would react.

What about you? Has faith in Christ made a difference in your life?

Or more importantly, have you ever asked the question, "What must I do to be saved?" This is the day of decision. Don't wait until your life is falling apart or you are at the point of ultimate despair like our jailer friend. Christ makes all things new! What does it mean to believe in Christ? It means believing that God loved the world so much that He gave His only Son, Jesus, to offer His life on the cross as the sacrificial payment for all our sins. It means believing He rose from the dead. Whoever believes in Him will not perish, but will have eternal life.

Joy begins here. Ironically, joy is found at the foot of the cross. What seemed like the most terrible punishment and death turned out to be the greatest source of hope for all mankind. There is no greater joy than knowing we are recipients of His grace and love. When we place our faith in Christ, we become a part of His family and partakers of His grace. Just as the jailer and his family rejoiced because they believed in Christ, we too can experience that purest form of joy by knowing we are a part of God's family and our sins are forgiven.

God-Sized Possibilities

We all find ourselves in unexpected twists and turns throughout our lives. It may not be a stinky prison cell, but it could be a sour marriage, an unfulfilling job, unfortunate diagnosis, or a rebellious child. Paul and Silas' surprise prison visit was no surprise to God. God was with them through this painful experience, and I want to reassure you of God's presence through your difficulties as well. Psalm 34:18 (NLT) reminds us that "the LORD is close to the brokenhearted and saves those who are crushed in spirit."

When I first started writing this book, I thought about making the title of this chapter "It Ain't Over Until the Jailer Sings." Aren't you glad that Paul and Silas didn't call it quits in the prison cell and respond to their circumstances with anger and despair? Instead of looking down in defeat, they looked up to God. They praised God because they knew that God was bigger than their situation, and their faith reminded them that God is a redeeming God. If God can bring joy from the horrible crucifixion of His Son, and if God can build the basis for the

Philippian church out of the deepest, darkest dungeon, then what can God do in your life?

Let's choose to look at our circumstances with expectancy and hope based on our faith in the God who loves us. Let's go the extra mile and praise God for what He is doing and what He can do beyond what we can see. He may not fix our situation with an abrupt earthquake, but don't put it past Him to shake up your world and bring about spectacular results. The word *serendipity* means unexpected pleasure. Let's be on the lookout for serendipitous moments when God surprises us with fresh possibilities in seemingly hopeless situations.

Personal Pursuit

ADDITIONAL READING: Acts 16—The Story of the Beginning of the Philippian Church

BASIC TRUTH: God is a redeeming God. He can take a bad situation and use it for good.

CHOICES:

- Trust God's love for you and His purpose for your life.

- Believe God can use difficult and challenging situations for good.

- Pray to God and praise Him in the midst of your challenges.

- Choose to respond to unexpected circumstances with faith and not fear.

- Be honest about your pain. Grieve your loss and allow God to comfort you.

- Remember other people are watching how you react to difficulties.

- Believe in the Lord Jesus Christ and you will be saved.

DELIBERATE PLAN: Remembering to Look Up

Stimulate your brain to develop a new habit of prayer and praise as your first reaction to difficulties in your life. Write on several index cards the following two questions:

1. Have I prayed about this?
2. Have I praised God?

Place the index cards in several places where you know you will see them during your typical day (near the bathroom mirror or in the laundry room, kitchen, and car) to help you continually remember to react in the same way Paul and Silas did in the dungeon. You may want to add a Bible verse at the bottom of the card. Perhaps Psalm 62:1-2 would be a good verse to use.

> I wait quietly before God,
>   for my victory comes from him.
> He alone is my rock and my salvation,
>   my fortress where I will never be shaken.

CHAPTER TWO

$\mathcal{P}$ardon My Progress

For we are God's masterpiece. He has created
us anew in Christ Jesus, so we can do the
good things he planned for us long ago.
—EPHESIANS 2:10

Of love there be two principal offices;
one to give, another to forgive.
—JOHN BOYS

You can't stop progress. Go to any major metropolitan city and you will most likely see several buildings undergoing improvements of some sort. You'll also see the familiar yellow tape cordoning off the construction zone with a sign reading something like, "Pardon Our Progress." Of course, we dutifully comply with the instructions on the sign and pardon or excuse the inconvenience because we are generally okay with a little progress here and there. Progress is a good thing, but the downside is it causes a disruption—maybe a detour—and a fair amount of mess to make the desired improvements.

If only we had the same grace toward people as we do toward buildings under construction. Wouldn't the world be a lovely place if we saw a small sign on each person stating, "Pardon My Progress"? That sign would serve as a constant reminder that people are continually growing and learning and in need of understanding. On the flip side, don't we wish others could see a little "Pardon My Progress" sign on our own hearts when we find ourselves in the place of needing to receive kindness, patience, or encouragement from them?

Progress in people can be messy. Sometimes God does His greatest work through our brokenness, weaknesses, or difficulties. One of our biggest challenges in life is to live with mercy and grace toward others as well as ourselves, recognizing that while we journey here on earth, we are in the construction phase. We will make mistakes. We will stumble and fall, but we can always learn, mature, and grow in the process. As Christians we are assured that God has begun a good work in us, and He will carry it on to completion until the day of Christ Jesus.

Paul saw the "Pardon My Progress" sign as he observed his precious and dear friends in Philippi. He was with the Philippians when the gospel first took root and began to grow in their hearts, and now ten years later, he is writing them a letter to encourage their strength and joy in the Lord. Quite a bit of construction took place in Paul's own life between the time he first met his friends in Philippi and when he wrote the letter we now read in our Bibles. During those ten years, Paul traveled down an extremely rough road. We can catch a glimpse of what his life was like by reading some of his other letters. Here again is another portion of his letter to the Corinthian church, most likely written about five years before his letter to the Philippians. I want you to read this to get a feel of what Paul's life was like after he left Philippi.

> We do not want you to be uninformed, brothers, about the hardships we suffered in the province of Asia. We were under great pressure, far beyond our ability to endure, so that we despaired even of life. Indeed, in our hearts we felt the sentence of death. But this happened that we might not rely on ourselves but on God, who raises the dead. He has delivered us from such a deadly peril, and he will deliver

us. On him we have set our hope that he will continue to deliver us, as you help us by your prayer.[1]

Did you read that? He despaired even of life! I think we could safely say that Paul was not living on Easy Street. Paul's life was messy, yet beauty blossomed through his difficulties. He said his challenges happened so that he and his companions would rely on God and not on themselves. He set his hope on God. He believed in God's ability to care for him because he experienced God's deliverance from deadly peril in the past. Paul grew strong in his faith through the challenging detours in his life. He didn't quit when the going got tough. He didn't give up on God or on others. Quite the contrary, he grew strong, he improved, and his faith increased.

At the beginning of his letter to the Philippians, we see that Paul wants the Christians of Philippi to recognize they too are under construction and God will continue to complete the work He began in their lives. God's work in them began when they came to a saving faith in Christ, and His work continues as He builds their faith and hope. The work will not be complete until they see Christ face to face. It's the same story in our lives as believers. Being under construction doesn't always look pretty, but as progress and improvements are made, we begin to get a glimpse of what the architect is doing, and our faith grows in the process.

A Beautiful Progress

Henrietta Mears saw the best in the people God placed in her life. Although her physical eyesight began to deteriorate at an early age, leading eventually to blindness, her insight into God's Word and her talent to see the potential in others grew in strength throughout her life. Born in 1890, Henrietta loved God's Word even as a child. She constantly begged her parents to let her go to the adult Sunday school classes at her church so she could learn deeper truths about the Bible. She taught her first Sunday school class when she was eleven years old. When Henrietta graduated from high school, her eye doctor warned her that she should not seek further education as it would strain what little eyesight she had left.

Henrietta didn't let the doctor's orders stop her. She was determined to use her eyesight until it was gone. She did her best to listen in class to reduce her need for reading. When she graduated from college, she went on to teach high school chemistry, but her first love was teaching the Bible at her church. Her classes grew in size as she taught God's Word with creativity and accuracy. Eventually she was invited to be the Christian education director at a Presbyterian church in Hollywood, California. She accepted the position and immediately began to write new curriculum to replace the old dull lessons she had been given. She wrote Sunday school lessons for first through twelfth grades, which eventually led her to start Gospel Light Publishers.

College students were her first love, and she faithfully taught their class every year. The students loved her because she taught such fun, quirky, and creative lessons. Henrietta helped them dream big dreams and catch the vision of what God could do in their lives. Hundreds of her students went on to full-time Christian ministry, including Bill Bright who founded Campus Crusade Ministries. Henrietta planted many seeds that God watered and grew into great and fruitful trees. She started a youth camp in California, which is now known as Forest Home Conference Center.

One year Henrietta invited a young evangelist to preach to the kids at Forest Home Camp. This young preacher was struggling with what he believed about the inerrancy of the Bible. Henrietta talked with him and prayed with him. Most importantly she didn't give up on him. She recognized that God was doing a great work in this young man's life and knew God would carry it out to completion. The preacher took a long walk in the forest and then got down on his knees, declaring to God that he would stand on the Bible as God's truth even if it didn't all make sense to him. Young Billy came back that evening to preach one of the most powerful sermons Henrietta had ever heard. Many kids came to trust Christ that very night. Billy Graham went on to preach his first crusade soon after his experience at Forest Home.

Billy Graham said that Henrietta Mears was one of the most influential women in his life besides his own mother and his wife. Aren't you glad Henrietta saw her students as works in progress? She didn't give up on them. She didn't focus on their faults. Rather she poured into them and nurtured them in the Lord. She reminds me of Paul. Henrietta wasn't imprisoned by being chained to a guard, but she was imprisoned by her physical blindness. Yet just like Paul, she didn't let her challenges keep her from building up others and encouraging them to be all that God wanted them to be. She looked for the potential and not the problems.

A Grateful Attitude

Take just a moment to think about the last time you sincerely encouraged another person. It may have been through a phone call, email, or a hug. It could have been a good word you gave a person during a short chat. Hopefully you don't have to think back too far before recalling a time when you took the opportunity to lift someone up. It's easy to encourage someone when things are going well, but imagine if your life was falling apart. Would you still be a fountain overflowing with cheer, strength, and comfort for others? I dare say that most of us want to be the recipient of encouragement, not the giver of it during our low points.

Imagine Paul chained to two prison guards, unable to come and go as he pleased. Yet there he was writing letter upon letter to encourage others. Honestly, I am moved by the kindness and affection that flowed from this man in chains to the people he dearly cared about. Now, it is a general principle in life that when we uplift others, we ourselves are uplifted. Paul certainly exhibited this principle in his words and in his actions. He sincerely loved the believers to whom he wrote, and I believe his encouraging words not only brought great joy to them, but to Paul as well.

As we roll out Paul's letter to the Philippians, let's first take a quick look at his thoughtful salutation. If you are like me, I tend to overlook these little phrases, but I want you to catch a little gem that reminds us of the work God was doing in Philippi. Paul opens his letter with these words.

Paul and Timothy, servants of Christ Jesus,

> *To all the saints in Christ Jesus at Philippi, together with the overseers and deacons:*

> *Grace and peace to you from God our Father and the Lord Jesus Christ.*[2]

Now I know it may seem like a small thing, but I think it is interesting to note that Paul is writing to the believers in Philippi along with the "overseers and deacons." Remember, this church experienced a meager start—a jailer and his family and a few women—and yet here we see they already have enough people to require overseers and deacons. Paul's letter to the Philippians is estimated to have been written ten years after he first visited them. So in ten short years, things are growing, people are congregating, and the church at Philippi is well organized! They are no longer just an eclectic handful of believers. I just wanted you to notice the progress they made since their messy beginning. Take heart! Their start wasn't so lovely and peaceful, but God was only beginning His work with them.

Next I want you to see how much the Philippians were continually and affectionately in Paul's thoughts and prayers. Here's how he built them up.

> *I thank my God every time I remember you. In all my prayers for all of you, I always pray with joy because of your partnership in the gospel from the first day until now, being confident of this, that he who began a good work in you will carry it on to completion until the day of Christ Jesus.*[3]   PHIL. 1:3—6

Think about how much those words must have meant to the early believers. Paul thanked God for them every time he remembered them. What about the people in your life? Do you thank God for them every time you remember them? I'm not talking just about the few easy-to-love favorites in your life; I'm talking about the more challenging people too. Let's be honest here. When we think of some people, we sometimes remember how they hurt or annoy us, we wonder what is wrong with them, and we make unfair comparisons. But thanking God for them? I'm not sure my heart and mind are always filled with thankfulness. What about yours?

What if we made it a practice to turn our minds from thinking negatively about the people around us (both the lovely and the difficult ones) to living with a continual habit of thankfulness for them? How would our relationships change? If we took our eyes off the negative and annoying qualities and began searching (yes, with some we may need to search a little harder than with others) for the positive qualities, we might begin to interact with people in a different way. But by taking it a step further, we could choose to thank the Lord even for the negative qualities because God uses those rough edges to do a work in our lives as well. When people are not so easy to love, we depend on the Lord to love them through us. Sometimes God uses the "sandpaper people" in our lives to smooth out some of our own blind spots and help us become a little less self-centered.

I must admit, in my own life, I can look back and thank the Lord for some of the challenging people because they have shaped my character and helped me to love in a deeper and richer way. Okay, I must also admit that I wasn't thankful for them at the time—case in point, my very first teaching job straight out of college at a middle school in Mesquite, Texas. I was hired as a seventh-grade math teacher and girl's athletic coach. You name it, I coached it—volleyball, basketball, track, and cross country. It was quite a busy year to say the least.

The middle school principal had a reputation for being, well, let's just say a little rough around the edges. He had been at the school for a gazillion years and didn't have a warm and fuzzy type of personality. I was little Miss Sunshine, and he was Mr. Thunderstorm. At the time I thought I had the worst teaching situation in the world. I didn't give thanks for him every time I thought about him. Nope, I pretty much thought God was punishing me by making me work for him.

Years later I can look back and say, "Thank You, Lord, for Mr. Thunderstorm because You used him to help me develop a thicker skin, grow up, and recognize that not everyone is easy to get along with.

Although some people are difficult, there is a person inside that rough exterior who needs Your love and forgiveness just as much as I do."

I believe I would have had a more positive first year of teaching if I had given thanks for him in the midst of my challenges. Actually by the end of that year, I did see evidence of a wise and thoughtful person inside that crusty exterior. He was there all the time. I just needed to take the time to look for him.

Who do you need to see in a different light? Is it a coworker, a neighbor, or a family member? It may even be your spouse. Let's make an intentional effort to thank the Lord for the people around us every time they come to mind, even the not-so-easy-to-love ones. Thank the Lord for the work He is doing in their lives and the good work He is doing in your life as well. It will make a difference to them, but more importantly it will make a difference in you. As you begin to replace anger and hurt with gratitude and joy, you will be transformed into a person who is rich in relationships and filled with love.

We must recognize difficult people are often hurting on the inside. Perhaps the reason they are annoying, unkind, or demanding is because they are dealing with past hurts and pains. Many people have wounded spirits, and we must remember to look past their masks or the rough exteriors and see a person who needs God's love. Ask the Lord to give you His perspective when you are dealing with a difficult person. We are all works in progress who need grace and love. May we be generous in pouring it out to the people God places in our lives.

A Deeper Fellowship

Trish couldn't believe it when her husband informed her that they were moving again. Two moves in three years was not exactly her picture of a perfect scenario to raise their kids, but if her husband was going to move up the corporate ladder, then they all needed to move along with him. It saddened Trish to know that her kids were forced to make new friends everywhere they went, yet the kids seemed to adjust fairly quickly to their new environments. Actually it was Trish who experienced a personal pain when it came to the turnover in relationships.

In each city Trish barely had time to make acquaintances with the other soccer moms in the neighborhood before it was time to pack up and move on. She longed to have a heart connection with a friend she could go to lunch with or call about the latest sale. She wanted someone with whom she could talk about life's issues beyond surface chatter, but she didn't know where to find this type of friend and didn't think it was possible with their nomadic life.

An old acquaintance recommended Trish check out some of the local churches in her new city. She did. All of her life, Trish had known about Jesus, but she had never come to a point of understanding what Jesus did on the cross. One day while listening to the sermon, she seemed to hear the gospel message for the first time. She began to understand the bigger picture, how Jesus offered His own life as payment for her sins and how He rose again, giving her the promise of eternal life. That very day Trish prayed a prayer of faith, believing in God's Son as her Savior. Soon the rest of her family believed as well.

Trish started to attend a local Bible study to learn more about this God who loves her. As she did, a heart connection began to build with the other women in the study. It was a deeper bond than she had ever experienced in the past. It was the true fellowship that comes from being sisters in Christ. The Bible says that when we believe in Christ, we become a part of His family, and God's Spirit comes to live within us.[4] Trish found that she now had sisters who would pray with her, encourage her, and strengthen her, and she could do the same with them too. What's more, she wasn't afraid of the next move because she knew wherever she went she could find other sisters in Christ with whom to form a bond.

As Christians, we have the common connection of being a part of God's family and partakers of His grace. There is a deeper fellowship between us. Our Christian bond should be much more than in name only because we share a connection of the heart and soul. Communities of believers ought to be filled with loving people, overflowing with grace toward one another. Unfortunately bitterness, pettiness, or gossip can easily seep into circles of believers and soon destroy the oneness that can be experienced in the body of Christ.

Paul offers us a pure example of heartfelt love between Christians. As we continue to read Paul's letter to the Philippians, his affection for them comes flooding forth. Surely the believers at Philippi already felt he cared for them from his words of thankfulness and his belief in their progress, but now he speaks from the depth of his being.

> *It is right for me to feel this way about all of you, since I have you in my heart; for whether I am in chains or defending and confirming the gospel, all of you share in God's grace with me. God can testify how I long for all of you with the affection of Christ Jesus.*[5]

Paul felt a true affinity with his fellow believers. He had them in his heart because they equally shared in God's grace. Paul longed to be with them to encourage them, yet he was prohibited by his chains. But distance didn't matter. He used terms of endearment to let them know how he felt. He told them he longed for them with "the affection of Christ." Oh, how I wish we all felt this way about each other as fellow believers in Christ. Think about the beauty we would show this world if we sincerely loved each other and longed for each other with the affection of Christ. What if we joyfully cared for each other's needs? What if we didn't argue with or complain about each other? What if we built each other up rather than tore each other down? Oh, how beautiful the body of Christ would be!

I am reminded of Jesus' words to His followers, "A new command I give you: Love one another. As I have loved you, so you must love one another. By this all men will know that you are my disciples, if you love one another."[6] As women who are recipients of God's grace, we share in a common fellowship with each other. We are a part of God's family and ought to share a bond of love for one another based on Christ's love for us. When the world looks at believers in Christ, they should be able to see a picture of what Christ's love looks like. I'm not so sure that's what they see right now.

Amazing Love

The affection of Christ is a powerful statement. Ponder for a moment the rich meaning of the term "the affection of Christ" and what it represents to us personally: Christ's love and passion for us. This amazing, grace-filled love brought Him to the cross where He offered His life on our behalf. As the glorious words from the hymn written by Charles Wesley proclaim, "Amazing love! How can it be that thou my God should die for me!"[7] Have you ever stopped to think about what Christ's love for us really looks like? Sometimes I think we forget how dearly loved we are as Christ's own people. His affection is not based on loving us because we deserve it. He loves us even when we don't deserve it. In the book of Romans, we catch a glimpse of the affection of Christ toward His people.

> Therefore, since we have been made right in God's sight by faith, we have peace with God because of what Jesus Christ our Lord has done for us. Because of our faith, Christ has brought us into this place of undeserved privilege where we now stand, and we confidently and joyfully look forward to sharing God's glory.
>
> We can rejoice, too, when we run into problems and trials, for we know that they help us develop endurance. And endurance develops strength of character, and character strengthens our confident hope of salvation. And this hope will not lead to disappointment. For we know how dearly God loves us, because he has given us the Holy Spirit to fill our hearts with his love.
>
> When we were utterly helpless, Christ came at just the right time and died for us sinners. Now, most people would not be willing to die for an upright person, though someone might perhaps be willing to die for a person who is especially good. But God showed his great love for us by sending Christ to die for us while we were still sinners.[8]

True love, wouldn't you say? We weren't attractive and worth dying for, yet while we were sinners, Christ suffered and gave His life for us. This is the affection of Christ. It is undeserved passion, love, and grace.

God showed this gracious love toward us, and now we, in turn, can be a reflection of this love to the people around us. It binds us together as believers, and it shines brightly to touch a hurting world. Jesus told us to love beyond easy love. He told us to love even our enemies. Anyone can love those who love them, but it takes the transforming love of Christ to love our enemies and do good to the ones who mistreat us.

The affection of Christ! Oh Lord, may Your people be visual examples of the passion of Christ as we display His love toward one another. Let the world see what it means to receive such amazing grace through the example of our grace-filled love toward others. Loving Father, pour Your love through us, so that we may transform the world with the affection of Christ.

A Passionate Prayer

My precious sister in Christ Thelma Wells prays with a powerful passion. She pours out her heart before the Lord in a way that moves me to tears and fills me with joy. Her passionate prayers are an overflow of her heart for God and her love for His people. She has a heart like Paul's toward the people of God as she gives her time and talent to encourage believers around the world through her books and speaking ministry. In fact, she even wrote a book titled *God Is Not Finished with Me Yet.* Sounds like Paul's words to the Philippians, doesn't it?

Known affectionately as "Mama T," Thelma has experienced her fair share of disappointments, frustrations, and difficulties in life, yet her faith in God is unwavering. The smile on her face is very real and sincere as she reaches out and touches people with His love. Whether she is speaking on a stage in front of thousands of people or praying with a few close friends, her passion for Christ shines so brightly you need sunglasses just to look at her!

How does she do it? How does she experience such joy in difficulties and boundless love toward others? She would be the first to tell you it's not her. It's God's Spirit at work in her. Her faith and love are strengthened as she looks to God to meet her needs. Thelma says, "Winning is not about brilliance or intelligence. It's really about humbling ourselves before the mighty hand of God, trusting in Him with all our soul and mind, forgiving ourselves and others for everything done to us, and seeking forgiveness for everything we've done to others. It's about keeping our mind on Jesus, walking in righteousness, understanding the truth of God, praying with all sincerity, being prepared with the Word of God in our spirit, and being covered by our unwavering faith in God."[9]

Our prayer life makes a difference in how we see life. When we pray with sincerity, as Thelma mentioned, our faith is strengthened, and our worrying is minimized. When we sincerely pray for others, our love for them grows. Yes, I mean it. As we lift others up before our loving heavenly Father and seek God's best for them, we can't help but come to a place of loving and forgiving them. God's love spreads throughout our hearts as we love people through prayer. How often do we sincerely pray for others? It's a good question to ask ourselves. Oh, we may *say* we are praying for people all day long, but do we really do it? Are we honestly lifting up others to our heavenly Father?

Paul thoughtfully and sincerely prayed for his Philippian friends, and I can't help but believe his love for them grew as a result. He tells them exactly how he was praying for them. As you read these words, I want you to think about the people in your life for whom you can pray a prayer like this.

> *And this is my prayer: that your love may abound more and more in knowledge and depth of insight, so that you may be able to discern what is best and may be pure and blameless until the day of Christ, filled with the fruit of righteousness that comes through Jesus Christ—to the glory and praise of God.*[10]

Paul began by praying for their love to abound more and more. Talk about a prayer God wants to answer! God desires His people grow in their love not only for Him but for each other. Certainly the greatest prayer we can pray for someone is that they would grow in the area of love. Observe what is entailed in the love Paul mentions in his prayer. He wants their love to abound in knowledge and depth of insight. This

recognize more, the real needs of others!

is much more than a fluffy love based on feelings. No, he is praying for a depth of love based on knowledge and insight.

Recently in the news, a celebrity couple went through a big messy breakup. What a shocker. The husband was interviewed on one of the entertainment shows, and he said he just didn't feel a love for his wife anymore. Instead he had fallen in love with his "soul mate." He added, "You just can't help who you fall in love with." Oh really? As if love is something you just haphazardly fall in and out of and can't help it. In his mind I guess he thought love is something that just takes you over in some mindless sort of emotional captivity.

True love, on the other hand, is based on knowing the object of our love and not simply floating in and out of love depending on how we feel. In the Bible we are commanded to love the Lord our God with all of our heart, soul, *mind,* and strength. To grow in love with God, we get to know Him through meditating on what the Bible has to say about Him. To grow in love with others, we must take a genuine interest in them. Sometimes we must deliberately stop thinking about our own stuff to pay attention to the needs of others. We all struggle with selfish tendencies, and we all need to intentionally step outside our own interests to truly see the needs of the other person. When we take the time to get to know the people in our life, our love is taken to a deeper level. We gain insight into what is important to that person. So the real question is how well do you and I know those we say we love?

Can I be brutally honest here? Often in relationships, I want people to know me and like me. I'm embarrassed to admit that all too often I don't take the time to learn more about the people I say I love. Of course, I enjoy the warm fuzzy feeling that comes from someone else loving me. Oh, how self-centered and shallow is my love! I'm convicted through Paul's words that I need to intentionally love people by getting to know them, their interests, their passions, and their pursuits. I can see why Paul prayed for the Philippians to love with knowledge and depth of insight because shallow love comes so very naturally.

Lord, help us to love one another with true depth, knowledge, and sincerity!

If we really get to know someone, then we will more likely be able to discern what is best. This is especially true in parenting. When we take the time to understand and know our children, we get to know what motivates them and what discourages them. Such knowledge can be helpful when it comes to disciplining our kids. I often see moms and dads parent out of fear, laying down all sorts of over-the-top rules to guard their kids from every evil known to mankind. Yet if they intentionally observed and got to know their child, they would know what rules are necessary and what types of punishment will be effective. Every child is different. If you are a parent, love your child by getting to know and understand them, so then, as Paul said in his prayer, "you may be able to discern what is best."

In his best-selling book, *The 5 Love Languages,* author Gary Chapman reminds us of the importance of getting to know the way people give and receive love. The more insight we have toward others, the more we can sincerely love and encourage them. Paul's passionate prayer serves as a model for us as we pray for others. Consider praying something similar to his as you lift up your loved ones.

> *Dear Lord,*
> *Please allow _____'s love for You and for others to abound more and more in knowledge and depth of insight, so that she (or he) may be able to discern what is best and be pure and blameless until the day of Christ. Allow _____ to be filled with the fruit of righteousness, which comes from Jesus Christ. And may this all be for Your glory and praise, wonderful heavenly Father. It is in the name of Jesus I pray, Amen.*

What a powerful prayer to pray for our loved ones! What a powerful prayer to pray for ourselves as well. We all need this prayer. May God allow our love for Him and for others to abound more and more in knowledge and depth of insight too. As we pray for others and get to know them better, our love for them will deepen and grow. Are you struggling to love someone right now? Pray for them and don't just pray that they change. Get to know them and bring out the best in them as you pray a prayer like the one we just read. We are all works in progress. God can give us patience and understanding during the construction phase.

The Power of Pardon

Never again say to yourself, "Oh, I'm such a failure." Never again whisper under your breath about another person, "Oh, she is hopeless. She will never get her act together." Don't give up on others and don't give up on yourself. Instead see each person as a work in progress. Progress is messy, but God is at work. He works in mysterious ways, and He doesn't work the way we think He should work. He doesn't answer to us, and He sees beyond what we can see. We want to fix people now, but God wants to do a mighty and eternal work in each of our hearts and lives.

Make a deliberate effort to see the sign on each person, "Pardon My Progress." Pardon is a powerful word. It means to exempt the guilty party; to forgive or to excuse. It's not an easy word to carry out in everyday life. Pardoning an offense against you or someone's mistake doesn't necessarily come naturally. As believers in Christ, we know the tremendous blessing of being pardoned from our sins because of what Christ did on the cross. Through faith in Him, we are forgiven. Because we have been so graciously pardoned from the penalty of our sin, we too must pardon others. Jesus said, "Do not judge, and you will not be judged. Do not condemn, and you will not be condemned. Forgive, and you will be forgiven. Give, and it will be given to you. A good measure, pressed down, shaken together and running over, will be poured into your lap. For with the measure you use, it will be measured to you."[11]

Be generous with pardons and stingy with condemnation. There is great joy in continually forgiving others and great pain in holding onto bitterness, anger, and resentment. Maybe you are not living in chains as a prisoner like Paul or trapped in blindness like Henrietta, but perhaps you are trapped in the prison of unforgiveness. When we do not pardon others, we place ourselves in a dark prison. Don't stay there.

With God's help, you can break through those bonds of bitterness that entrap you. Consider right now if there is anyone you need to forgive and seek God's help in the process. He's an expert at forgiving.

Sincere love and pardoning go hand in hand. When I consider how Paul defined love, I see the beauty of forgiveness shining through. Here's his description.

> Love is patient, love is kind. It does not envy, it does not boast, it is not proud. It is not rude, it is not self-seeking, it is not easily angered, it keeps no record of wrongs. Love does not delight in evil but rejoices with the truth. It always protects, always trusts, always hopes, always perseveres. Love never fails.[12] I COR. 13:4-8
> (UNCONDITIONAL)

If our love is to abound more and more for one another, we must begin with a spirit of continually pardoning others. Pardoning doesn't mean you invite someone to walk all over you or do something awful to you again. You may need to set healthy boundaries if a person is taking advantage of you. We must continually pardon in order to live our lives free of bitterness and anger. Ultimately the Lover of our souls, the perfect Pardoner can give us what we need to sincerely love and forgive others. Look to Him and thank Him for pardoning you, and ask Him to help you and give you strength to pardon others.

═══ *Personal Pursuit* ═══

ADDITIONAL READING: Romans 5 and 8—God's Great Love for Us

BASIC TRUTH: God began a good work in each one of us and is not finished with us yet.

CHOICES:

- Thank the Lord for all the people in your life, both difficult ones and pleasant ones.

- Realize progress usually entails messiness, challenges, and detours.

- Always keep in mind that everyone is a work in progress.

- See yourself as a work in progress as well. God's not finished with you yet.

- Love others with the affection of Christ.

- Pray for others' growth and strength in the Lord.

- Practice continual forgiveness and pardoning.

DELIBERATE PLAN: The Thankfulness Project

Choose a 24-hour period where you will deliberately give thanks for everyone who comes to mind. Thank the Lord for their good qualities, and thank the Lord for the qualities that help you grow as a person. Use this as an opportunity to let people know how thankful you are for them. Write them a note or email or give them a call to tell them that you thanked the Lord for them. As you thank the Lord for others, ask Him to bring to mind anyone you need to forgive. Seek God's help in forgiving and pardoning others.

$\mathcal{D}$iamonds Formed Through Difficulties

*My life is an example to many, because you
have been my strength and protection.*
—Psalm 71:7 NLT

*Our troubles have always brought us blessings, and they
always will. They are the dark chariots of bright grace.*
—C.H. Spurgeon

It's not easy to teach junior high kids. As a former math and science teacher, I constantly tried to infuse creative and innovative ideas to keep the attention of my young students. Hands-on experiments always worked much better than the lessons out of the textbook, so we did all sorts of crazy fun science labs. We made rock candy out of sugar water. We created weather vanes out of drinking straws and cardboard. We planted, we baked, and we measured to experience the lessons. I probably shouldn't mention the story about the gerbils we had in the front of the classroom and the horrific day when the mama gerbil ate one of its babies right in the middle of my math lesson. I never knew seventh-grade girls could scream so loud.

Despite the cannibalistic gerbil escapade, we actually had quite a few amusing lessons as a result of our science experiments. Petri dishes, especially, offered a good opportunity to grow all sorts of things. Mold was always an ooey-gooey favorite of the junior high kids. Of course, it isn't necessary to be in a science classroom to grow things like mold. It grows quite quickly on the leftovers in my refrigerator without a problem. Yes, given the right environment, mold just takes off without any effort on my part. I only wish the plants in my garden would grow that easily!

It's amazing to realize we can grow so many substances given the right set of circumstances, yet there are some things that do not grow so easily. Take diamonds for instance. I'd love to do a little science experiment and grow some diamonds, wouldn't you? Diamonds are simply carbon crystals, and so you would think they would be as easy to grow as rock candy, salt crystals, or mold. Unfortunately it's just not that simple to grow a diamond. The truth is diamonds only form under conditions of intense heat (2200 degrees Fahrenheit) and immense pressure (usually formed between 75 and 120 miles under the earth's surface), so I'm thinking I am out of luck trying to grow a diamond in my kitchen or the science classroom. Mold, yes—diamonds, no.

Now if you had the choice between becoming a gleaming diamond or a green mold, which would you choose? I'm pretty sure I know the answer to that question. Without a doubt, most of us would rather be lovely, glowing, brilliant diamonds rather than yucky, ugly mold. A diamond is a true treasure, not easily formed and not easily found. Diamonds are stunning in appearance, bringing joy to those who wear them and those who see them. Diamonds are also considered one of the hardest substances in the world. Some drill bits are made from diamonds and are used to cut through other rocks. Vibrant, valuable, and strong, yes, that's what I want to be!

Yet let us not forget that diamonds must go through intense heat and immense pressure to form their valuable qualities. Often our beautiful qualities are formed through the heat of trials and the pain of afflictions.

I wish it weren't so! I would love to be a strong, courageous, wise, godly woman through peaceful, lovely, mellow experiences in life. Wouldn't you? But, alas, the tribulations and challenges grow us, teach us, inspire us, and mature us. Mold grows in nice happy environments—diamonds grow through difficulties. As we learned in the previous chapter, Paul knew what trials looked like. He even came close to death several times, but he chose to see his trials as treasures. He chose to look at the good that came from his challenges, both in his own life and in the lives of others. We too can choose how we will view our circumstances in life. Will we embrace the challenges, or will we whine and cry for a petri dish type of life?

Brilliant Shine

Being a prisoner can take the wind right out of your sails. Paul had a great ministry before he was sent to jail. He was making an impact in people's lives and helping to start churches all throughout Asia and Europe. He was doing God's work, preaching the gospel everywhere he went and building up the body of believers. It wasn't like he was some sort of scoundrel or thief who deserved to be imprisoned. Nonetheless, he ended up in prison once again, this time in Rome, chained to a palace guard. Now, some people would become bitter and start grumbling and complaining if they found themselves in a similar situation.

Paul's eyes weren't on his dismal circumstances. They were on what God was going to do despite the challenges. Instead of wishing away the situation, Paul chose to discover possibilities of hope right where he was placed. He even wanted to reassure the Philippians that God was using his bad circumstances for good. Here's what he wrote next in his letter.

> *Now I want you to know, brothers, that what has happened to me has really served to advance the gospel. As a result, it has become clear throughout the whole palace guard and to everyone else that I am in chains for Christ. Because of my chains, most of the brothers in the Lord have been encouraged to speak the word of God more courageously and fearlessly.*[1]

Let's be up front and real here. Sometimes it is just plain hard to see the good in the middle of our not-so-great scenarios. It could be that we just don't feel like looking for what is good, or it may be that we can't seem to find even an ounce of good that could come out of our difficult circumstance. In either case we are in need of God's help. We need Him to shine His light on our dark moments and help us see His presence in our situation. We may not be able to envision how anything good could come from our circumstances, but we can look to the God of hope. The situation may seem hopeless, but God has not left us. With our eyes on Him, we begin to see life differently.

Consider Shandra's story. Shandra was a businesswoman in a Southern coastal town. She was having a hard time being around her friends and coworkers because she was a Christian, and they did not share her beliefs or lifestyle. She felt lonely and wanted to give up many times, but, instead, she decided to consult her pastor.

The wise pastor asked her a question. "Where do we put lights?" he asked.

Puzzled by the silly question, she responded, "We put them in the dark places of our house." In that moment she understood what he was trying to say and realized God had put her in those difficult surroundings so that she might shine for the Lord. She began to experience joy and courage whereas before she had felt frustration and fear. After several weeks had passed, Shandra arrived at church with a group of joyful young women. Yes, God did an amazing work through Shandra at her work place, and many of her coworkers came to know Christ through her example, her words, and her radiant joy.[2]

"Appearances can be deceptive. The fact that we cannot see what God is doing does not mean that he is doing nothing," says the great theologian Sinclair Ferguson.[3] Paul was also stuck in a dark situation, but he caught a glimpse of hope. He recognized that God could do great things despite his imprisonment. God used Paul's time in chains to inspire and encourage others to boldly shine God's light. Perhaps you are wondering how Paul ended up in prison again. The whole adventure (and it really is quite a story) can be found in the latter part of the book of Acts, but I'll give you a short summary. When Paul was in Jerusalem, some of the Jewish leaders did not want him to preach the gospel, so they had him arrested. Paul eventually appealed to Caesar, which meant it was necessary for him to go to Rome. Through shipwreck and peril of many kinds, Paul finally made it to his destination in Rome.

The Treasure of the Trials

In Dallas we have a tremendous amusement park called, "Six Flags over Texas." I loved to go to the park as a kid and loved taking my own kids to the park as an adult. Through the years we watched the park change quite a bit. As a grown-up, I would often drag my kids over to the big map that had the red arrow with a note reading, "You are here." Most of the time when I looked at the map, I realized the ride we wanted to go to was on the other side of the park. That's when I'd just look at the big red arrow and say, "I don't want to be here; I want to be there!"

Sometimes we may want to say that very same phrase about our life. Circumstances change in life and often end up far from what we planned or hoped for. I can imagine Paul was tempted to think to himself, *I don't want to be here in chains. I want to be out there, spreading the gospel and encouraging the churches.* At least I know that's what I would have been thinking, but Paul had a different attitude. He saw his chains as a good thing. Paul was under house arrest at the time he wrote to the Philippians, which was a little different picture than his experience in the stocks in the dungeon of the Philippian jail we read about in chapter one. We read in Acts 28:16, "Paul was allowed to live by himself, with a soldier to guard him," yet he still wasn't living in freedom.

He was able to dictate letters, receive visitors, and even preach the good news about Jesus to those who gathered at his home. The palace guard, to whom Paul referred in Philippians, was also known as the Praetorian guard. They were a distinct group of imperial guards, not a part of the Roman army or police. Isn't it almost humorous to picture these important guards chained to Paul? They didn't have a chance! They couldn't help but hear the message of God's love and grace through Jesus Christ because they were a captive audience. What a unique way for the gospel to spread in Rome! We know from Paul's parting words in his letter to the Philippians, God's Word even spread to those "who belong to Caesar's household," implying some of the guards followed Christ.

Where has God placed you? It may not be where you wanted to be or where you had planned to be, but I want to assure you that you are not there by accident. You are there for a purpose. No matter how you got there or where you are, God can do mighty things through you. Instead of complaining, arguing, or being frustrated, ask God to show you how He can use you right there in the place He has put you. Turn your eyes on the God of hope and turn your eyes off of your disappointments. Even if you made a mistake or unwise decision, God can work within it. Interestingly, if Paul had not appealed to Caesar, he would have been released at an earlier time and would have not gone on to Rome. Paul could have wallowed in regret about appealing to Caesar, but instead of seeing his appeal as a mistake, he focused on the blessing. What about you? You may be in your circumstances due to a bad choice or mistake. Thank God for His work beyond your mistakes or your limitations. Look with hope and expectancy at what God can do through your experiences to bless and strengthen others.

Inspired by Courage

Paul's courage while in chains gave courage to other Christians to speak more fearlessly. Personally, when I see the example of courage lived out in others who serve Christ, I too am encouraged to live more courageously and boldly. Elizabeth Gurney Fry is one of those inspirations to me. Born into a wealthy family in England in 1780, she enjoyed the finest parties England had to offer. Although Elizabeth's mother died when she was only 12, her family lived a colorful yet shallow lifestyle. When Elizabeth was 17, she was deeply moved by a message from a preacher named William Savery. Inspired and convicted by the gospel message, Elizabeth began opening her eyes to the needs of the poor and forgotten people of England.

She married Joseph Fry when she was 20 years old, and although she began to have children of her own (she eventually had 11 children), she took time to visit the slums of London and cared for the needs of the poor while also teaching them from God's Word. After learning about the terrible conditions for women who were in prison, Elizabeth bravely went to visit Newgate Prison. At first the guards wouldn't let her go inside because it was too dangerous. The guards themselves would never go in alone because the prisoners were known to be a wild mob. Elizabeth could have easily given up, but God put a determination inside of her.

After receiving permission from the governor of the prison, Elizabeth courageously entered the prison. There she found herself surrounded by 300 screaming women who acted like animals, clawing, scratching and fighting each other. Their conditions were deplorable as they were crowded together in four small cells. They were dirty, and some were almost naked. There were even children of prisoners dwelling there. Elizabeth wisely showed no fear, but rather went over and picked up one of the children and told the women they should all do something to help the children in their midst.

Elizabeth could have looked down on these women with disgust, but instead she chose to reach out to them in love. She began to teach them from God's Word, beginning with Isaiah 53:6 (KJV), "All we like sheep have gone astray; we have turned every one to his own way; and the LORD hath laid on him the iniquity of us all." She helped the women understand that Christ loved them and came to this world to forgive sin. Her desire was for the prisoners to come to a point of sensing a love and respect for God as well as for one another. She taught them how to knit and sew and started providing materials for them so they could even earn money.

She went on to speak to the House of Commons, beginning a movement for prison reform. Elizabeth never stopped thinking about those who were suffering. After hearing about a homeless boy who had died on the streets, she began to reach out and start committees to set up shelters for the hungry and homeless. She started more than 500 libraries for coast guardsmen and also started a school for nurses. Phew!

This woman never gave up! She had a passion for Christ and for people, and she had the boldness to carry out her mission.

Are you inspired by Elizabeth's story? Yes, I know you might be worn out by the thought of all she did, but on the other hand, it makes you realize how much one woman can do when she chooses to courageously live out her passion. The apostle Paul fearlessly lived out his passion for Christ by inspiring many others to preach the Word of Christ more courageously and fearlessly. Passion ignites courage, and courageous acts cannot help but inspire others. What are you passionate about? What motivates you and touches your heart? Prayerfully consider taking a courageous step forward in pursuing your God-given passion and making a positive difference in someone else's life.

Like it or not, our lives serve as an example to other people. Elizabeth Fry left her comfort zone, and because of her example, an entire nation was inspired to love and respect the downtrodden. Paul proclaimed Christ, fully knowing he could face imprisonment, yet he inspired fellow Christians who faced similar persecution. What about you? What has God put in your heart to do? It may not be easy. It may take courage. It may need to wait for a season, but begin seeking God's guidance to strengthen you, equip you, and direct you to carry out your passion in the place He has put you. You never know how your courage may inspire others to follow and serve Christ.

Mr. Positive

Recently a well-known congressman passed away. The news media stopped covering other news and devoted their time to create footage to honor this man's life. In my mind, I must admit, I was thinking that he did not deserve all of this glory and attention. Sure, he had served in congress for many years, but he also had a pretty shady past and even did some things he publicly regretted. His funeral and all the procession that went with it was featured on every major network station for hours. It bothered me. Then a friend told me she watched the entire funeral, and despite disagreeing with this man's political ideology, Christ was proclaimed at his funeral.

It was a reminder to me that the message of Christ is ultimately what is important, not my viewpoints or opinions. I don't need to waste time judging motives. Instead I need to do what God has called me to do and share the message of Christ's love. As I heard about the funeral, my mind jumped to Philippians and the very passage I have been contemplating. Paul reminded his fellow believers of the same type of lesson I learned from my friend. Here's what he wrote next in his letter to his Philippian friends.

> *It is true that some preach Christ out of envy and rivalry, but others out of goodwill. The latter do so in love, knowing that I am put here for the defense of the gospel. The former preach Christ out of selfish ambition, not sincerely, supposing that they can stir up trouble for me while I am in chains. But what does it matter? The important thing is that in every way, whether from false motives or true, Christ is preached. And because of this I rejoice.*[4]

Paul rejoiced that Christ was preached despite the false motives or basic disagreements. Talk about Mr. Positive! Once again, he chose to look at the upside and keep his eyes on the goal of spreading the gospel. I'm amazed at how petty we Christians can get over little issues that don't matter, arguing over assumptions, motives, or disagreeing on issues that in the big scheme of life just don't matter. We need to take a cue from Paul and drop it. Apparently some Christians were trying to use Paul's imprisonment to their advantage, further their own ministries for selfish reasons, and tear down Paul's reputation.

Paul didn't want competition between ministries to become an issue. For him, the cause of Christ was the only issue that mattered. Let's stop being critical of other ministries just because they compete with or look different than ours. Instead of working against each other to entice the most members or followers, wouldn't it be lovely if churches and ministries worked with each other to encourage all people to come to Christ? The love between believers and the unified purpose of the body of Christ should be a beautiful example of what the body of Christ ought to look like to the rest of the world.

It is interesting to note that Jesus discussed this same issue when He was on earth with His disciples. Let me take you to the scene. The disciples had been arguing about which one of them would be the greatest. A little prideful one-upmanship was taking place within the group. Can't you just picture each disciple bragging about how he deserved to be the greatest in God's kingdom right in front of Jesus? Jesus decided to have an intimate conversation with them about this matter. He told them, "If anyone wants to be first, he must be the very last, and the servant of all."[5] Well now, that's a little different than our normal way of thinking.

Jesus then brought in a child and said, "Whoever welcomes one of these little children in my name welcomes me."[6] Jesus was teaching them the importance of reaching out to the little ones, not only those whom society deems important and significant, which is a vital lesson for us all, but Jesus wasn't finished with the lesson yet.

John, the beloved disciple, piped in, "Teacher…we saw a man driving out demons in your name and we told him to stop, because he was not one of us."

The disciples still couldn't get over the competition thing! If the disciples struggled to this extent with self-serving interests, what hope is there for us? We all need to hear the Master's words and continually reflect on what really matters. Here's Jesus' response to John's question. "Do not stop him…No one who does a miracle in my name can in the next moment say anything bad about me, for whoever is not against us is for us. I tell you the truth, anyone who gives you a cup of water in my name because you belong to Christ will certainly not lose his reward."[7]

Although we need to be discerning, we don't need to waste time judging or speaking against one another. Other groups, ministries, or organizations may not look like ours, but God has given each one different gifts, talents, and personalities. If the truth of Christ is preached, then let's guard ourselves from speaking negatively. I'll be the first to tell you I don't like some of the Christian stuff we see on television. I question their motives and methods, but I must admit I have met people who while in the depths of despair turned on their television in the middle of the night, heard a television evangelist, and came to a saving faith in Christ. So I listen to Paul's words once again. "The important thing is that in every way, whether from false motives or true, Christ is preached. And because of this I rejoice." The focus is on Christ, not on self.

By saying all of this, I do want to add one word of caution. We must be discerning and careful about where we place our financial support and who we endorse. There are those who deceive and those who are corrupt in the ministry, so be wise. Jesus warned His followers to be aware of wolves in sheep's clothing and those who may look good on the outside but are corrupt within. Let us rejoice when Christ is preached, but let us also be guarded against scams, scavengers, and those who are using the gospel to line their pocketbooks. Before you send support, always check out a ministry to make sure your donation is being used for kingdom purposes and not selfish ones. A good resource to discover the financial integrity of a ministry is Evangelical Council for Financial Accountability. Go to www.ecfa.org for more information.

Stop Judging. Start Living!

It is safe to say we all tend to waste a little too much time judging and condemning others when we should be doing what God has called us to do. Paul wasn't proclaiming that motives aren't important and that it's okay to drive forward with self-ambition. He was telling us to keep our eyes on what matters most and leave the judging to God. I know I need to regroup every day to make sure I am focused on what matters most. It's so easy to get distracted by assumptions, worries, selfish ambitions, and comparisons that don't really matter in the big scheme of life.

As we passionately pursue Christ, we must lay the distractions aside. Like a runner in a race who must shed anything that would keep him from running well, we must shed both sin and distractions that can keep us from running with victory and endurance. The writer of Hebrews talks about the life race we are running. He reminds us to throw off that which weighs us down. He also tells us to keep our eyes on what matters most.

> Therefore, since we are surrounded by such a great cloud of witnesses, let us throw off everything that hinders and the sin that so easily entangles, and let us run with perseverance the race marked out for us. Let us fix our eyes on Jesus, the author and perfecter of our faith, who for the joy set before him endured the cross, scorning its shame, and sat down at the right hand of the throne of God. Consider him who endured such opposition from sinful men, so that you will not grow weary and lose heart.[8]

When our eyes are on Jesus, we are focused on what really matters. How do we combat the jealousy, selfish ambition, and rivalry that may take place in work, ministry, or life? We fix our eyes on Jesus, the author and finisher of our faith. We run the race He set for us, leaving the comparisons behind. This is our encouragement and our strength, to look to Jesus our example, who for the joy set before Him endured the cross and scorned its shame. He is now seated at the right hand of the throne of God in the position of honor and power.

In this race of life, what keeps us from living for Christ and shining His light for the world to see? It may be the drive to be appreciated, recognized, accepted, have expensive things, or be involved in a bunch of activities. All of these can distract our focus on Him. Let us run our race with our eyes on the Lord. Don't compare yourself to others. He has equipped you in a unique and wonderful way to shine His light and be a beacon of hope to others no matter where you are, what you have, or what you don't have.

Is the race easy? It rarely is! Endurance and perseverance are required, but remember diamonds aren't formed in lovely, comfortable, cushy scenarios. We may not have the luxury of choosing our circumstances, but we do have the opportunity to choose our viewpoint and outlook. Instead of focusing on his chains, Paul focused on the fact that the gospel was being advanced. Instead of wallowing in self-pity because of his confinement in Rome, he rejoiced because other Christians were encouraged by his example to be bold and speak about their faith. Instead of being consumed by comparisons to other ministries and judging motives, Paul chose to rejoice in the fact that the gospel was being preached. He was focused on the goal! Where's your focus?

Personal Pursuit

ADDITIONAL READING: Acts 24–28—Paul's Journey to Jail in Rome

BASIC TRUTH: We can choose to trust God and embrace our challenges, or we can choose to despair and become discouraged.

CHOICES:

- Recognize diamonds are formed under intense heat and immense pressure. Mold is formed in perfect and comfortable environments.

- Look for the good in every situation.

- Ask God to help you see what you can be thankful for in tough times.

- Learn from courageous examples. Be a courageous example.

- Live with passion for Christ.

- Serve others and let go of selfish ambitions.

- Rejoice when Christ is preached.

- Be cautious of deceptive practices in ministries.

- Run your own race and don't compare it to others.

- Focus on Christ and not on comparisons or difficulties.

DELIBERATE PLAN: Courageous Examples

Consider some of the courageous examples you have observed throughout your life. It may have been a godly grandmother, a girl who stood for Christ in high school, or a coworker who suffered because he or she did what was right. On the lines below, write their names and thank the Lord for their influence in your life.

JEAN (& PAUL) FILPUS

_____

_____

_____

_____

_____

_____

You may want to study some of the courageous women in the Bible, such as Ruth, Deborah, Hannah, Elizabeth, or Mary. Ask the Lord to allow you to be an example to others as you passionately pursue Him.

CHAPTER FOUR

_Living Your Life with Passion and Purpose

Since, then, you have been raised with Christ, set your hearts on things above, where Christ is seated at the right hand of God. Set your minds on things above, not on earthly things.

—COLOSSIANS 3:1-2

All to Jesus I surrender,
All to Him I freely give;
I will ever love and trust Him,
In His presence daily live.

—JUDSON W. VAN DEVENTER

When is the last time you sobbed with reckless abandon while watching a movie—I mean the kind where you were embarrassed to leave the theater because your makeup was streaking down your cheeks? As I have grown older, the list of the movies that moved me has grown longer. Of course, any movie where a horse or a dog dies always grabs me. I absolutely couldn't make it through *Marley & Me*. I even cried at the end of *King Kong* because the big ape was so misunderstood. Hero tales mixed with love stories are movies where I can't control my tears, especially if the hero dies for the sake of his beloved.

At the top of my list of movies that make me bawl uncontrollably is, of course, *The Passion of the Christ*, produced by Mel Gibson. I cried so deeply that I couldn't catch my breath, and I was afraid I would make one of those loud gasping noises right there in the middle of the theater. The movie powerfully and graphically portrayed Christ's suffering and death, and as a follower of Christ, I couldn't help but be overtaken with emotion. *The Passion of the Christ* is the ultimate heroic love story, and it is even more overwhelming to think about the fact that *we* are the beloved for whom He died.

As I left the theater at the end of the movie, I, along with everyone else who had just seen the movie, walked out in total silence. It was almost eerie. I thought to myself, *I will always live with a passion for Christ.* In the days after the movie, I still kept thinking about the vivid pictures of Christ's suffering. Weeks and months went by, and the pictures began to fade in my mind, and soon I was back to my busy life filled with trivial pursuits. Can you imagine if we lived each day with our hearts filled with thankfulness for what Christ did for us on the cross? How different would our relationships be if we focused on Christ's sacrificial love for us? What actions would be different in our lives if we were consumed with the love of Christ?

The truth is movie memories can't sustain our personal passion for Christ. God can certainly use a movie to stimulate our desire for Him, but it is God's work in us that draws us and strengthens our passionate pursuit of Him. The apostle Paul lived with a singular focus on Christ, and the same Spirit who lived within Paul dwells within every believer. Let's take a look at his declaration of passion and reflect on what we can learn from his devotion.

> *I eagerly expect and hope that I will in no way be ashamed, but will have sufficient courage so that now as always Christ will be exalted in my body, whether by life or by death. For to me, to live is Christ*

and to die is gain. If I am to go on living in the body, this will mean fruitful labor for me. Yet what shall I choose? I do not know! I am torn between the two: I desire to depart and be with Christ, which is better by far; but it is more necessary for you that I remain in the body. Convinced of this, I know that I will remain, and I will continue with all of you for your progress and joy in the faith, so that through my being with you again your joy in Christ Jesus will overflow on account of me.[1]

Paul's life was defined by Christ. For Paul, to live was Christ! Jesus gave Paul's life meaning and purpose. His sole reason for living was to bring the joy of Christ to others. Yet Paul was also okay with dying for the cause of Christ. In fact, he was leaning toward being in heaven with Christ as the better option. He didn't cling to the things of this life because he didn't cling to this life at all. Now don't get me wrong, he wasn't depressed and suicidal; he just lived with an eternal focus. He knew the best part of his life was yet to come in heaven with Christ. The reason he desired to live in this world was to continue his work of spreading the gospel and encouraging believers.

Cling-Free Living

Jennifer has a long road ahead of her before she finishes medical school. As a senior in college, she's already been through quite a few grueling hours of study, but she continues to keep her eyes on the goal. Jennifer has worked each summer, watched her spending, and remained disciplined, knowing there are better days ahead. She knows her life as a student is temporary, and she is living in anticipation of that day when she can put on her white coat and proudly add the letters M.D. to her name.

Paul lived with that same type of anticipation, but instead of a doctor's white coat, he was looking forward to wearing the white robe of righteousness believers in Christ will receive in heaven one day. Knowing the temporary status of life here on earth, Paul was able to live with open hands. Instead of clinging to the things that only provided fleeting fulfillment, he clung to Christ, his all in all. It's funny how we tend to believe that certain people or situations hold the key to our happiness when, in reality, these things do not provide lasting and true satisfaction.

Paul didn't hold onto the things of this life (reputation, possessions, people) with a tight fist. He held it all with an open hand. He appreciated what God had given him, but he wasn't dependent on or devoted to them. He didn't live with attachments to this world; he lived with an attraction to the next. What would our lives look like if we simply appreciated the people and objects of this world but lived full throttle for Christ with our hearts and minds set on eternity?

Here are the results I picture:

- more sincere love and care for others; less self-centeredness
- more encouragement and kindness; less arguing and bickering about petty stuff
- more giving to those in need; less hoarding and keeping for ourselves
- more peaceful and calm hearts; less worrying and anxiety
- more sharing the gospel; less concern about what people think
- more prayer; less gossip
- more God-honoring actions; less people-pleasing ones
- more building up others in their work and ministries; less tearing down and jealousy
- more joy; less grumbling

What would you add to the list? Think about what this world would look like if we, as women who follow Christ, lived cling-free lives. Instead of grabbing hold so tightly to the trinkets this world has to offer, we would be wise to release our grip and live in the freedom and joy of our heavenly citizenship. I often picture the simplistic monkey traps used by primitive tribes. You know the ones that were simply a jar with a small opening and a banana in the bottom. When the poor unsuspecting monkey reaches into the jar to grab the banana, he becomes entrapped because he won't let go of his grasp of the bait. Personally, I must consider what it is that I won't loosen my tight grasp on and, therefore, entraps me. As I write this chapter, I am convicted of areas in my own life to which I have clung a little too tightly. What are you holding onto with clenched fists?

Oh Lord, open our eyes to see what we are clinging to. Gently, patiently, mercifully help us to release our grips and open our hands to You, trusting You. Set our eyes on what is to come, recognizing that our best life is not here, but there. Strengthen us for the journey and help us to live beyond the temporary with our hearts set on eternity.

When our passion is to seek God and know Him more, we will not be disappointed. There is nothing more satisfying than drawing close to God and growing to love Him in a deeper and more real way. All other pursuits or passions will eventually disappoint. People will let us down. Objects will not live up to their invitation. Drugs and alcohol will only lead to a desire for more. But our loving and faithful God will not disappoint. Psalms reminds us that God "satisfies your desires with good things so that your youth is renewed like the eagle's." The psalmist goes on to tell us "The LORD is compassionate and gracious, slow to anger, abounding in love."[2] Now, don't you want to get to know a God who satisfies our desires and is abounding in love?

C.S. Lewis, in his message titled "Weight of Glory," wrote, "Our Lord finds our desires not too strong, but too weak. We are half-hearted creatures, fooling about with drink and sex and ambition when infinite joy is offered us, like an ignorant child who wants to go making mud pies in a slum because he cannot imagine what is meant by the offer of a holiday at the sea. We are far too easily pleased."[3] God is offering us a pleasure that satisfies our deepest desire—the pleasure of knowing Him—but often we are trying to amuse ourselves with unsatisfying trinkets.

A Chance to Die? *(God's "COLLATERAL DAMAGE"* 🎀)

If someone were to write a biography about your life, what title would best describe your story? Have you ever thought about it? I would want my life described with fun and upbeat words in the title like *The Fascinating and Joyful Life of Karol Ladd* or *Adventures in Living Life to Its Fullest: A Story about Karol Ladd*. Hmmm…I'm not so sure how many copies that would sell. Maybe my family and a few close friends would buy a copy, but I'm not even sure about that.

Can you imagine the title of your biography being *A Chance to Die: The Life and Legacy of Amy Carmichael? A Chance to Die* is not one of those bright, fluffy titles that we would love to describe the tenure of our lives; nonetheless, it is a book filled with the fascinating stories and adventures about a woman who lived with a singular focus and a passion for Christ. Amy Carmichael was sold out to the Lord, devoted to prayer, and committed to serving Christ through helping others in need. She was a woman with depth of insight and a desire to live for God wherever He called her.

Born in 1867 in Northern Ireland, Amy developed a compassion for people at a young age and had a true sense of social concern. At the age of 17, she began teaching a Sunday school class to the girls who worked in the local mill in Belfast. The class quickly grew to over 500 ladies, yet at the age of 24, Amy felt God calling her to the foreign mission field. She began her missionary work in Japan with a fervent desire to win souls for Christ, but after 15 months, she had to leave Japan due to illness.

Like Paul, Amy didn't allow a few little interruptions to stop her from spreading the gospel. Eventually her missionary work took her to India, and it was there she became aware of the terrible plight of the young girls sold into temple prostitution. Amy soon became known as *Amma* (the Tamil word for "mother") because she courageously began to take in and protect children who had been sold into child prostitution.

In her later years, Amy suffered a serious fall that left her unable to resume her normal activities. Although she was physically limited, her ministry continued to grow. She wrote numerous books during this time in her life when she wasn't able to get out and about. God used her mightily to inspire countless others to draw close to Christ and live for Him. Elisabeth Elliot was one of those women whose life was impacted by Amy's example. It was from Amy's book titled *If* that Elisabeth first started to understand the great message of the cross and of what Amy called "Calvary love."

Elisabeth went on to write Amy's biography, *A Chance to Die.* (I highly recommend you read it.) In the introduction Elisabeth wrote, "I saw that the chance to die, to be crucified with Christ, was not a morbid thing, but the very gateway to Life. I was drawn—slowly, fitfully (my response was fitful), but inexorably. In a far more secular and self-preoccupied time Amy Carmichael's vision of the unseen and her ardent effort to dwell in its light, making any sacrifice for its sake, seems hardly believable, let alone worth trying to imitate."[4] Elisabeth Elliot went on to imitate Amy's life in many ways, courageously bringing the gospel to the Auca Indians, the very people who killed her husband.

"Amy Carmichael set her face toward that other Country," proclaimed Elisabeth.[5] Amy herself wrote in a letter, "'Hereby perceive we the love of God, because He laid down His life for us, and we ought to lay down our lives for the brethren.' How often I think of that *ought.* No sugary sentiment there. Just the stern, glorious trumpet call, OUGHT. But can words tell the joy buried deep within? Mine cannot. It laughs at words." Amy knew a deeper, indescribable joy of the heart and the satisfaction that comes from a complete surrender to God and obedience to Him. No one could take that joy away from her. Although she never married and did not enjoy many luxuries this world has to offer, Amy experienced an immutable satisfaction.

One evidence of her commitment to Christ is found in a document Amy drew up titled "Confession of Love." She wrote it for a group of Indian girls who banded together to serve Christ, and here we catch a glimpse of what Amy believed about pursuing Christ with passion.

> My Vow: Whatsoever Thou sayest unto me, by Thy grace I will do it.
>
> My Constraint: Thy love, O Christ, my Lord.
>
> My Confidence: Thou art able to keep that which I have committed unto Thee.
>
> My Joy: To do Thy will, O God.

My Discipline: That which I would not choose, but which Thy love appoints.

My Prayer: Conform my will to Thine.

My Motto: Love to live—live to love.

My Portion: The Lord is the portion of mine inheritance.

Teach us, good Lord, to serve Thee as Thou deserves; to give and not count the cost; to fight and not to heed the wounds; to toil and not to seek for rest; to labor and not to ask for any reward save that of knowing that we do Thy will, O Lord our God.[6]

What a beautiful picture of a heart sold out to Christ. Like Paul, she had an eternal focus and a singular purpose. She also knew where her joy and satisfaction came from. Read back through her "Confession of Love" one more time and ponder a life lived with a passion for Christ. After I read Amy's "Confession of Love" several times as well as the prayer that follows, I decided to make a copy and carry it with me in my daily planner. I try to consistently use it as a bit of a reminder and a self-check. Is my vow to do whatever He says to do by His grace? Is my joy to do His will? Is my prayer to conform my will to His? Amy's "Confession of Love" is convicting and motivating at the same time. It is a reflection of what a life lived passionately for Christ looks like.

True Passion

When you think of the definition of the word *passion,* what comes to mind? I usually think of passion as a strong feeling, affection, or emotion about something or someone. A woman who is passionate pours herself wholeheartedly into a cause, a person, or an experience. Yet if you look up the word *passion* in the dictionary, you will find a rather surprising definition. In *Webster's New World Dictionary,* the original definition is, "suffering or agony, as of a martyr." The second definition reads, "the agony and sufferings of Jesus during the Crucifixion or during the period following the Last Supper."[7]

Hold on now. Wait a minute! I thought *passion* was a happy word like *zeal* or *enthusiasm.* I must admit I was shocked when I read the definition of *passion* and realized it referred to agony. The root word comes from the Latin *passus,* which means to endure or suffer. We see the same root in words like *patience* and, of course, *compassion* (with suffering). That's why the portrayal of Christ's journey to the cross is called "The Passion of Christ." Now I get it!

What Christ did for us on the cross defines passion. He willingly left the glory of heaven and came to this earth to offer His life for us. He suffered and endured the pain because He had a greater purpose, a purpose to die on our behalf. May we never take it for granted! When we talk about someone living with passion, we really ought to refer to someone who is willing to endure and suffer for the purpose for which they feel called. At this point you may be thinking you would like to lay this book aside (or throw it in the trash) and shout, "I give up! I will never be a woman who passionately pursues Christ because I don't want to suffer!"

Honestly, who does want to suffer? Even Jesus while in the garden of Gethsemane asked the Father to remove this cup from Him. Yet He prayed, "Not my will, but yours be done."[8] A passionate pursuit of Christ takes us to a place where we are willing to say, "Father, I want what You want." You may feel inadequate or unable to pray that prayer. I know I do. The apostle Peter struggled over and over with some of these same issues. Interestingly, even Peter seemed to want what he wanted for Jesus, and suffering wasn't in the picture. Do you remember in the story of Jesus when He proclaimed to His disciples that He was going to suffer and die, Peter was the one who took Him aside and rebuked Him. Peter had a different idea of who Jesus should be. He saw Him as a glorious king, not a suffering servant. Jesus had some strong words in return for Peter. He said, "Get behind me, Satan!…You do not have in mind the things of God, but the things of men."[9]

Peter wasn't so different than you and me. He simply preferred to avoid suffering. Remember his denial of Christ not once, not twice, but three times? But Peter was a work in progress, just as we are. God began

His work in Peter, and He continued to allow it to grow and flourish into a life lived passionately for Christ. What was his secret? I believe we find the key to his passion as we read the beginning of one of his letters. He said, "By his divine power, God has given us everything we need for living a godly life. We have received all of this by coming to know him, the one who called us to himself by means of his marvelous glory and excellence. And because of his glory and excellence, he has given us great and precious promises. These are the promises that enable you to share his divine nature and escape the world's corruption caused by human desires."[10]

Living a life of passion for Christ is God's work in us. He began a work in us, and He will carry it on to completion. By God's divine power, He has given us everything we need for living a godly life. So we look to Him and seek to get to know Him more deeply and purely. As we do, He will lead us through the valleys and carry us through the deep waters when they rise. He will begin to exchange our feeble desires toward the things of this world with the satisfying desire of knowing Him.

Singular Focus

Recently I attended a conference led by Anne Graham Lotz (Billy Graham's daughter). The title of the event was "Just Give Me Jesus." Anne desires nothing more than to be used by God to bring people to the cross. In fact, the stage itself was void of decorations and distractions. There was only one item that graced the stage, and it was a wooden cross. The focus of the conference was Christ alone. I'm sure most of the women who attended the event went home with a deeper desire to know Him more, to surrender all, and live for Him.

Just listening to Anne Graham Lotz was a refreshment for the soul. Her life message and singular focus was clear, "only Jesus!" Here is a woman, like Paul, who is sold out to Christ. Her whole desire is to see people come to Christ. She is not distracted by competing ministries, petty issues, or trying to make a name for herself. Her joy is found in her Savior. Although her life is not always easy, her eyes are on Jesus, and she finds her strength at the foot of the cross. Like Amy Carmichael, Anne's example encourages and inspires me. The same Spirit who is at work in Anne's life and in Paul's life and in Amy Carmichael's life is also at work in your life and in my life.

In his book *Absolute Surrender,* author Andrew Murray reassures believers that it is God who does the work within us. God gives us the willingness to surrender as well as the ability. Here's what he wrote.

> God does not ask you to give the perfect surrender in your strength, or by the power of your will; God is willing to work it in you. Do we not read: "It is God that worketh in us, both to will and to do of his good pleasure?" And that is what we should seek for—to go on our faces before God, until our hearts learn to believe that the everlasting God Himself will come in to turn out what is wrong, to conquer what is evil, and to work what is well-pleasing in His blessed sight. God Himself will work it in you.[11]

Only by God's Spirit at work within us can we desire to live for Christ. Only by His Spirit can we live without distractions and with a singular focus on Him. The secret of a passionate pursuit is a humble heart that prays, *Have mercy on me a sinner, O God. I do not desire You as completely as I should. I get distracted by all that is in this life. Help me to have a heart for You. Please give me more of Jesus and less of me.*

With humble hearts let us go to God and seek His help not only to have the power to center our lives on Him, but also the desire. God's invitation to us is always, "Come." Dwight L. Moody said, "I know of no truth in the whole Bible that ought to come home to us with such power and tenderness as that of the love of God."[12] With arms open wide, God invites us to recognize His great love for us and His desire for deep and abiding relationship with us. Deeper still! Oh, may our love for Christ go deeper still.

Whatever Happens

Paul didn't try to sugarcoat the Christian life. He was open, honest, and real with the Philippians, offering encouragement to them as they faced their own difficult times for the cause of Christ. He offered them some words of strength as they were facing some of the same struggles Paul had experienced. Here's what he said.

> *Whatever happens, conduct yourselves in a manner worthy of the gospel of Christ. Then, whether I come and see you or only hear about you in my absence, I will know that you stand firm in one spirit, contending as one man for the faith of the gospel without being frightened in any way by those who oppose you. This is a sign to them that they will be destroyed, but that you will be saved—and that by God. For it has been granted to you on behalf of Christ not only to believe on him, but also to suffer for him, since you are going through the same struggle you saw I had, and now hear that I still have.*[13]

When Paul used the words, "whatever happens," it reminds me that we have no guarantees as to how our life will turn out. We do not have the comfort of knowing that our circumstances will be happy and blissful. We have no entitlement of a life of luxury or fun, but we do have the comfort of knowing God will be with us and will give us what we need. Despite the circumstances, with God's help we can conduct ourselves in a manner worthy of the gospel of Christ. What does the term "worthy of the gospel of Christ" look like in a practical sense? To me it means allowing the love and forgiveness of Christ to pour out from my heart and bless other people. It means not living in fear, but leaning on God's strength and wisdom through my struggles. As David proclaimed:

> Even when I walk
>   through the darkest valley,
> I will not be afraid,
>   for you are close beside me.
> Your rod and your staff
>   protect and comfort me.[14]

God's presence through our struggles is what offers us comfort. Do not be afraid. Your good Shepherd is close beside you. He will not leave you in the deep waters or storms of life. *He will deliver you on the Other Side!*

Paul actually used a bit of a strange word to let the Philippians know they would probably go through some struggles. He said it has been "granted" to them on behalf of Christ, not only to believe on Christ, but to suffer for Him. Now, typically when something is granted to another person, it is something good. When a student receives a grant for school tuition, it is a wonderful gift. When a nonprofit organization receives grant money, it's a great blessing. When a citizen is granted an audience with the president, it's a tremendous opportunity. But being granted the opportunity to suffer? That's not where I would use the word *granted*.

Can suffering be considered a gift from God? It may be too difficult to think about it in those terms. Much of the cruelty and pain we see in this world is a direct result of sin and the evil that dwells here. But it is possible to look at suffering and see God has allowed it, even granted it for a good purpose. The message of the gift of suffering is found consistently throughout the Bible. You may not see the message of the gift of suffering in a lot of popular Christian books, and you don't hear it proclaimed from many pulpits. Let's be honest—it's not a "feel good" message. But as we observe the trials of Joseph, the lamenting of Jeremiah, the difficulties of Daniel, and the persecution of Paul, we can't help but see God had a great purpose in granting the opportunity to suffer. Of course, the ultimate picture of the gift of suffering is our Lord Jesus, who faced the brutal death on the cross only to be resurrected from the dead, providing hope and forgiveness for all who believe.

James wrote, "Consider it pure joy, my brothers, whenever you face trials of many kinds, because you know that the testing of your faith develops perseverance. Perseverance must finish its work so that you may be mature and complete, not lacking anything. If any of you lacks wisdom, he should ask God, who gives generously to all without finding fault, and it will be given to him."[15] So even though we don't go looking for suffering, when it does happen in our life, we can choose to respond in a positive way. We can receive it with joy, knowing that God is doing a greater work in us. More importantly we can seek God's wisdom and direction on how to grow, learn, and make it through. He invites us to ask.

Will you join me on a pursuit, a passionate pursuit like Paul's? He ran his race with his eyes fixed on Jesus, letting go of all the stuff that would hold him back from running his course. We don't have to become a missionary to be passionate for Jesus. We can passionately live for Him right where we are. With any race, we must recognize that it won't be easy. It may become grueling at times, but it is also a race filled with joy, a euphoric joy that no one can take away from you. It's a race worth running and a goal worth pursuing. For you understand that when we cross the finish line of this world, we have the glory of eternity to look forward to, and it is there that we will dwell with no more suffering and no more pain. We will be in the glorious presence of our mighty God, our good Shepherd, our Prince of peace.

Personal Pursuit

ADDITIONAL READING: 2 Peter 1-3—Guidance and Hope for Followers of Christ

BASIC TRUTH: Passionately pursuing Christ may be difficult, but there are great rewards as we persevere, grow, and look toward our future home.

CHOICES:

- Set your eyes toward eternity and not on the attractions of this world.
- Appreciate the people and things the Lord has given you.
- Ask the Lord to help you recognize areas in your life you are clinging to with clenched fists.
- Seek His help in holding these things with open hands.
- Get to know Him intimately by spending time alone with God in prayer.
- Passionately pursue Jesus and draw close to Him.

- Receive suffering with joy, knowing God is doing a greater work in you.
- Seek His wisdom, direction, and guidance through the suffering.

DELIBERATE PLAN: Defined by Christ

Just as Paul's life was defined by Christ, so we too must consider what defines our life. If you were going to briefly describe what defines your life right now, what would you say?

_____

_____

_____

_____

_____

_____

_____

As we personally and passionately pursue Christ, He begins to define our life more and more, and the things of this world define it less and less. How do we pursue Him? We begin by getting to know Jesus Himself. I would encourage you to read the Gospel of John slowly and steadily, just a little bit each day. Study Jesus' claims about Himself. Get to know how He treated others and how He acted and lived. No matter how long you have been a follower of Christ, it is a good idea to study the Gospel of John, taking a few verses at a time. Start a Jesus journal to record what you learn about Jesus in each passage and write out your prayers as well.

CHAPTER FIVE

The Surprisingly Delicious Flavor of Humble Pie

Worship the LORD with gladness.
Come before him, singing with joy.
Acknowledge that the LORD is God!
He made us, and we are his.
We are his people, the sheep of his pasture.

—PSALM 100:2-3 NLT

Humility in every area of life, in every relationship with
other people, begins with a right concept of God as the one
who is infinite and eternal in his majesty and holiness.

—JERRY BRIDGES

The drive from Dallas, Texas, to Pekin, Illinois, is a long one, especially for the kids in the backseat of the family car. Trust me, I know. As a child, our family made the trek from Dallas to Pekin at least once a year to visit my grandparents. Even though I didn't exactly embrace the long car ride, I did enjoy the small, hometown atmosphere of Pekin. It was a welcome change from the big city. I have fond memories of going to the park for picnics and riding in the paddleboats on the pond near the giant historic gazebo. I loved visiting the 4-H fair and playing bingo with my grandparents' friends on warm summer nights. I also loved my grandmother's home cooking, often made from the fruits and vegetables straight from her garden.

Although her pies were especially delicious, I must admit there was one I refused to eat. It was the rhubarb pie. I don't know why, but the thought of eating rhubarb just didn't seem appetizing to me. The name reminded me of some type of prickly wire used for a fence. Plus, have you ever seen a stalk of rhubarb? It looks like red celery. Not in my wildest dreams could I imagine how something that looked like celery could be good in a pie! I know it's silly, but I was a kid and didn't know any better. It wasn't until I was in my thirties that I decided to be brave and give rhubarb pie a try. You guessed it. I tried it, and I liked it! It has a unique, sweet and sour taste. I liked it so much I even began baking rhubarb pie, bread, and muffins.

It's funny how something may seem scary and awful to us until we actually get to know it. Then we see that it's not so bad after all. For me, humility has always been a scary concept. It was one of those principles in the Bible that I kind of slid right over and didn't really focus on during my Scripture reading. I certainly didn't want to pray for humility because I was afraid of what God might do to me to teach me its finer qualities. That's why I never prayed for patience either! Yet as I read how Paul described humility to the Philippians, it doesn't seem so awful anymore. It actually seems like a beautiful thing, a quality I honestly want to have in my life.

In Preparation for Humility

When you think of the word *humility,* what comes to your mind? As women, sometimes we are prone to think of humility in terms of putting ourselves down or as a form of self-hatred, self-doubt, or self-depreciation. Notice how many times I used the word *self* to describe the faulty concept of humility. The truth is humility has nothing to do with self and everything to do with God and our concept of Him and recognizing His power and sovereignty. Humility also has to do with thinking of others with no focus on ourselves. If you have ever asked yourself, "Am I being humble enough?" then you are asking the wrong question, and your eyes are looking in the opposite direction. Humility looks up and out—not in. When our concentration is on loving God and loving others, humility begins to grow.

Paul exhorted the Philippians to have a humble attitude, but he laid a little groundwork before he gave them this charge. Here's how Paul gently moved in the direction of addressing the topic of humility.

> *If you have any encouragement from being united with Christ, if any comfort from his love, if any fellowship with the Spirit, if any tenderness and compassion, then make my joy complete by being like-minded, having the same love, being one in spirit and purpose. Do nothing out of selfish ambition or vain conceit, but in humility consider others better than yourselves. Each of you should look not only to your own interests, but also to the interests of others.*[1]

Notice Paul opens four phrases in the same way by using the words, "If any…" I don't want us to miss these truths that lay a foundation for a humble attitude.

If you have any:

- encouragement from being united with Christ
- comfort from His love
- fellowship with the Spirit
- tenderness and compassion

As I read these four statements, it occurred to me that Paul assumed believers in Christ already had these blessings present in their lives. He was reminding the Philippians of the benefits they should be enjoying. We too ought to be enjoying these very same gifts from God, so as followers of Christ, we must ask ourselves:

1. Am I encouraged by being united with Christ, and am I strengthened by His presence in my life?

2. Am I personally experiencing comfort from His love day by day?

3. Do I have fellowship (a meaningful and vibrant relationship) with His Spirit?

4. Do I have a heart filled with tenderness and compassion toward others?

Take a moment and think honestly about each of these four questions. These are precious gifts from the Lord, and as followers of Christ, they are ours. Yet, doesn't it seem as though many of us as Christians are not living in the beauty of these blessings? On the contrary we are often: *(LACKING IN OUR CONVICTION!)*

- discouraged by the circumstances of life rather than encouraged by being united with Christ

- fearful and anxious rather than comforted from His love

- feeling frustrated and alone rather than experiencing the fellowship with the Spirit

- full of bitterness and anger rather than tenderness and compassion

What has happened to us? Why are we so far from experiencing these good gifts from God's grace? I don't think there are any easy answers. Perhaps we have become so distracted by the cares and worries this world offers that we have forgotten the comfort and joy that God offers. It may be that we have grown dependent on ourselves or others to meet our needs rather than depending on God's help and the fellowship of His Spirit to carry us through our challenges. Maybe we have forgotten the tenderness and compassion God shows us, and so we don't reflect it in our relationship toward others. Whatever the reason, I do think one step we can take is to recognize and acknowledge what God has given us.

Think about the example of David, a man after God's own heart, who said, "I will extol the LORD at all times; his praise will always be on my lips."[2] David was a man who lived with an attitude of praise and thankfulness to God as well as a humble reassurance of God's presence in his life. David accomplished great things for God, but he also had an abiding relationship with God. Clearly, as we look at David's life, we recognize he was:

- constantly encouraged by God's presence in his life
- comforted with God's love and found his hope in Him
- strengthened by fellowship with God's Spirit
- filled with tenderness and compassion toward others

Like David, let's enjoy the benefits of being a part of God's family and a partaker of His grace. We too can praise Him and thank Him for these blessings, and we can also ask God to renew and strengthen some of these elements of our faith in our daily lives. As Christians may we be people who genuinely are encouraged from being united with Christ, comforted from His love, experiencing the fellowship with the Spirit, and filled with tenderness and compassion. These are foundational fruits of our Christian life, and from these precious qualities flow a genuine spirit of humility.

Paul used these fruits to begin his "if…then" conversation. He told his fellow believers that since they were experiencing these glorious benefits, then they should be like-minded, having the same love and being one in spirit and in purpose. As Paul talked about being one in spirit and in purpose, we can assume he was referring to the powerful purpose of living for Christ and knowing Him. When we are sincerely walking in the light of God's love with a common goal of living for Christ, we will be at one with other believers. Why? Because we are not looking out for our own interests, but rather those of Jesus Christ and the people He has placed in our life.

Oh, Lord, draw us back to You. Help us to experience the joy of our salvation, the wonder of Your love, and the comfort of Your presence in our lives. As we experience more of You, let us live in unity with our brothers and sisters in Christ. May we be like-minded, one in spirit and in purpose, and focused on the glory of the gospel of Christ and not our own glory.

Looking Out for Others

There are certain attitudes within the body of Christ that can be destructive instead of constructive. Paul calls out two attitudes that seem to lead us away from humility rather than toward it. He warned, "Do nothing out of selfish ambition or vain conceit." When a woman is out for number one and is centered on her own self-advancement, there will most likely be disunity in the community. Personally, I used to think that women didn't exhibit much selfish ambition or vain conceit. I thought these were mainly guy traits. I found out how wrong I was the first time I signed up to help teach vacation Bible school at our church. I just wasn't aware that certain women staked their claim on both the age group they wanted to teach as well as who they wanted on their team. The underlying competition for the most gloriously decorated room, over-the-top games, and treats for the kids were additional matters.

It became evident to me that these women weren't in this to teach the gospel of Christ. They were there to show off their creative talents so that everyone could see how amazingly gifted they were. Fortunately kids still came to know Christ, but I'm glad the kids didn't see the spirit of one-upmanship that consumed many of the teachers, not to mention the jealous whispers taking place behind the scenes. I didn't know church ladies could be so ruthless. Selfish ambition shows up everywhere, and women's church groups are no exception.

The root of selfish ambition is the spirit of trying to get ahead of others for your own personal interests. It often includes pushing down others to elevate self. Gossip is a subtle form of selfish ambition. Instead of considering other's needs, a woman with selfish ambition is focused mainly on her own needs. Vain conceit is an ugly stepsister to selfish ambition. The opposite of our own vain conceit or vain glory would be God's glory. Are we doing things so people will look at us and say, "Wow, you are amazing"? Or do we do things with God's glory in mind, hoping people will say, "Wow, isn't God amazing"?

J. Oswald Sanders said, "The world has yet to see what could happen if everyone lost the desire to get the glory. Wouldn't it be a marvelous place if nobody cared who got the credit?"[3]

To a certain extent, I believe we all struggle with seeds of selfish ambition and vain conceit. Even women who always seem to be down on themselves are actually overly concerned about self. Let's admit it. We all have a self-centered sinful nature deep inside our glowing exterior. I must admit that even when I do something kind for others, I secretly want a little acknowledgement. I have a feeling you do too. Wanting a pat on the back is not necessarily a bad thing (although we certainly don't want it to be our primary motive), but it gets out of hand when we try to push others down to get what we want or cause disunity because our motive is for our own glory.

Our motives may never be 100 percent pure, but that's what keeps us in a place of dependence on God—a place of humility. There will always be that tension between our personal drive and our desire to glorify God in all we do. I don't believe we will ever be at a point where we can say, "Now I've got this pride and self-centeredness thing under control. I won't ever struggle in this area again." There is a slight bit of humility lacking in that statement, wouldn't you agree? Recognizing our own personal struggle with self-centeredness brings us to our knees before a loving God and encourages us to seek His help in loving others and honoring Him.

Humility is a heart issue. The condition of our heart can strengthen our ability to fight off the infection of pride that so easily dominates our thoughts and actions. When I use the term *heart,* I am referring to our focus and our passion, not just an intellectual acknowledgment. Three conditions of the heart seem to lend themselves toward humility: a heart of prayer, a heart of gratitude, and a heart of compassion. As these three attitudes permeate our lives, we begin to think and act differently. We begin to live with less self-centeredness, and we develop a God-centeredness and sincere love for others.

Prayer

A self-sufficient person says, "I can do it myself." A humble person says, "I need God." Peter, who learned a lesson or two about depending on God, wrote this, "All of you, clothe yourselves with humility toward one another, because God opposes the proud but gives grace to the humble. And God will exalt you in due time, if you humble yourselves under his mighty hand by casting all your cares on him because he cares for you."[4] So how do we humble ourselves under God's mighty hand? By casting all our cares on Him because He cares for us! When in humility we prayerfully bring our requests to God, we acknowledge our need and dependence on Him. Also as we pray, our minds are freed up from our own burdens, and we can more openly and honestly think about others.

Gratitude

George Herbert wrote, "O Thou who has given us so much, mercifully grant us one thing more—a grateful heart." When we live with a continual attitude of thankfulness, we recognize that all we have comes from Him. We don't take the glory for ourselves when we do something good or wise or noteworthy. Instead we are grateful to God for giving us the ability and the opportunity to do well. A grateful heart gives credit where credit is due, but if we fail to thank God, we begin to think we did it all by ourselves and pride sneaks into our thinking. Sincerely thanking God is a work that takes place in the quiet place between just you and Him. It brings us to a place of strength in Him and takes our focus off of ourselves.

Compassion

When Paul told the Philippians, "In humility consider others as better than yourselves," he was not instructing them to put themselves down, but rather he was telling them to lift others up. Paul wasn't in any way saying that the Philippians should think about others in a busybody type of way either, but rather in a caring and loving type of way. He went on to instruct them to take a genuine interest in others, not just think about their own interests. We all need to be reminded of this because being consumed with our own life and the things going on there is so easy. We must make a deliberate effort to step out of our own little world, reach out to touch others, and feel their pain. When we take the time to stop concentrating on our needs, our eyes begin to open to the needs around us. Each day, let's determine to bring sunshine into someone else's life by taking the time to think about their needs and showing them we truly care.

The Ultimate Example

Recently I was teaching a women's Bible study in downtown Dallas on the topic of humility. The Bible study was set up for working women who could walk from their workplaces in the downtown skyscrapers to a meeting place, enjoy a nice lunch, and hear a message from God's Word. When the ladies arrived, they walked through a buffet line to pick up their lunches and then sat down to listen to the lesson. For this particular lesson about humility, I decided to put on an apron and a cap to serve the women from the buffet line. Some of the women recognized me immediately. It took others awhile to realize I was serving them their lunch instead of greeting them in the front of the room dressed in my cute "teacher outfit." Everyone seemed to get a kick out of my unexpected role. When it was time for me to teach the lesson, I went to the front of the room and taught in my lunch lady outfit, which was much more comfortable to me than high heels anyway.

It was my intention for the women to be surprised by my switch in duties and clothing. Although these business women were used to seeing me teach the lessons every week in my nice, dress-up clothes, I wanted them to catch a glimpse of someone unexpectedly taking on a role of service. On a much grander scale, that's what Christ did for us. He could have come to this earth in majesty and power, strength and glory, and pomp and circumstance, but He chose, instead, to come as a servant. Jesus was the ultimate example of true humility, putting others' needs before His own. I am overcome with gratitude as I read the next portion of Paul's letter.

Your attitude should be the same as that of Christ Jesus:
   Who, being in very nature God,
      did not consider equality with God something to be grasped,
   but made himself nothing,
      taking the very nature of a servant,
      being made in human likeness.
   And being found in appearance as a man,
      he humbled himself
      and became obedient to death—
      even death on a cross!
   Therefore God exalted him to the highest place
      and gave him the name that is above every name,
   that at the name of Jesus every knee should bow,
      in heaven and on earth and under the earth,
   and every tongue confess that Jesus Christ is Lord,
      to the glory of God the Father.[5]

Jesus is the ultimate example of true humility! In Him we have the perfect picture of someone who did not think of His own needs but considered the needs of others more important than His own. Jesus did not claim His rights but rather gave them up willingly.

Thank You, Lord, for showing us in a very real and tangible way what the beauty of humility truly looks like! Thank You, Lord, for humbly offering Your life on the cross on our behalf. Thank You, Lord, for the gift of Your life. We are forever grateful!

Although Jesus was by very nature God, He didn't consider equality with God something to be grasped. By using the word *grasped,* Paul didn't mean Jesus couldn't reach or take hold of His heavenly rights. The word *grasped* would be better understood as "cling" or "grab with a clenched fist." Jesus had all the rights of equality with God, but He didn't cling or hold onto His deserved rights with a clenched fist but came to this world in human form. Jesus was all God and all man. It kind of blows your mind, doesn't it?

The point is Christ demonstrated humility by not grabbing and clinging to what He rightfully deserved. This is possibly one of the most difficult concepts for us to apply in our own lives. Often we—unlike Jesus—focus on our rights and cling to what we think we deserve, holding them with clenched fists, sometimes afraid to let them go. Here's a list of a few of the rights we tend to believe we deserve:

- I deserve a happy life.
- It's my right to get back at him or her.
- I deserve to be treated better by my subordinates at work.
- I have a right to yell at the kids because they deserve it.
- I deserve to have a loving husband who makes a good income.
- I can take this extra money from payroll because I deserve it.
- It is my body, and I have a right to have an abortion.
- After all I've done for him, I deserve better than this.
- I've worked here a long time; I have a right to take this.
- I've given a lot of money to this organization; I deserve to be heard.
- They have more than they need; I have a right to have some too.

Possibly the two most common ones are:

- I have the right to be mad at ____(insert person's name)____ .
- I have the right to have ____(insert something you want)____ .

There are times when we may even demand our rights with God:

- I go to church every Sunday, and so I have a right to a nice life.
- I fasted and prayed, and so I deserve to have this prayer answered like I want.

- I tithe my income, and so I deserve to be financially blessed.
- I have always been kind to the poor and needy, and so I don't deserve to lose my job.

The list could go on, but the point is that we all tend to demand our own way instead of prayerfully and humbly giving up certain rights. When we demand our rights or become focused on what we think we deserve, then we will live lives of frustration, anger, bitterness, and defeat. Yet if we are willing to give up our rights, we bless and bring peace to others and to ourselves. We experience a great joy when we give up what we think we deserve to help or bless others. Probably the toughest right we must give up is the right to hold something against another person.

Forgiveness means, "I release the right to hold this offense over another person." Christ gave us the example on the cross when He said, "Father, forgive them; for they know not what they do." Throughout the Bible, we as believers in Christ are commanded to forgive as the Lord forgave us. Yes, forgiving others is the greatest form of humility. In the quietness of your heart right now, I want to encourage you to consider if there are any areas in your life where you are clutching to your rights or demanding what you think you deserve. Are you willing to pry your fingers off of those rights and prayerfully ask God to give you wisdom on how to handle the matter?

In life, of course, there is always a balance. There are certain areas you should *not* lay down your rights. You do have a right to a safe home, and so in an abusive situation, you need to get help. When it comes to society, you do have the right to speak up against injustice, and I would encourage you to use that right carefully, wisely, and lovingly. The most wonderful right we have as believers in Christ is the right to approach the throne of grace in prayer and ask our loving heavenly Father for help.

Christ gave up the majestic treatment He deserved to take on the very nature of a servant. We can observe His servant's heart throughout His time here on earth. One of the most lovely pictures of servanthood

Christ gave us was when He took off His outer robes, tied a towel around His waist, and lovingly washed His disciples' dirty, stinky feet. This was a job saved for the lowest servants because it was not at all pleasant. In fact, it was probably pretty nasty. Those leather sandals didn't prevent road dust and street grime from getting between the disciples' toes, yet in an act of humility, Jesus knelt down and served His disciples.

Washing stinky feet doesn't even compare to the ultimate act of service Christ did for us. Death on a cross was usually reserved for the most notorious criminals, yet Jesus humbled Himself by becoming obedient to the worst sort of death—nailed to a cross! Crucifixion was extremely shameful and excruciatingly painful, but Jesus was willing to give up His rights and die on the cross for your sins and mine. Because of His willingness to endure a painful and shameful death on our behalf, God exalted Jesus to the highest place and gave Him the name that is above every name.

Christ Above All

There is no one else. Christ was exalted to the highest place. He came in humility and service, willingly offered His life, and now sits at the right hand of God in a place of honor and power. He is the One who gave His life, and He is the One who everyone will confess as Lord. Every knee will bow to Him in heaven, on earth, and under the earth. As we read the description of Christ's humility, let us not miss the important and eloquently professed message of Christ's authority. Consider the truths we glean about Christ in Paul's passage about humility.

- Jesus Christ has always existed with God.
- Christ is in very nature God.
- Christ became a human man.
- He willingly offered His life on the cross.
- God has exalted Him to the highest place.
- Christ's name is above every name.

- One day every knee will bow to Him.
- One day every tongue will confess that Jesus Christ is Lord.

As we ponder these proclamations, this question cannot be avoided: Do you believe them? Christ's name is above every name. He has been exalted to the highest place, and there are no others. We will either confess that Jesus Christ is Lord and Savior before judgment day or after. Right now we have a choice to willingly confess Christ as Lord. We also have the painful option of being forced to acknowledge His deity when we face judgment. The Greek word for *confess* (*exomologeo*) means "to profess or acknowledge openly; to affirm or agree." Paul wrote to the Romans, "If you confess with your mouth, 'Jesus is Lord,' and believe in your heart that God raised him from the dead, you will be saved."[6]

Have you come to a point in your own life where you have confessed and acknowledged that Jesus Christ is Lord? In the book of Revelation, there is a passage that makes me think about Paul's words to the Philippians. It is a picture of things to come, when all of creation will proclaim that Jesus Christ is Lord. Here are the words the apostle John wrote about the revelation of things to come.

> Then I looked and heard the voice of many angels, numbering thousands upon thousands, and ten thousand times ten thousand. They encircled the throne and the living creatures and the elders. In a loud voice they sang:
> "Worthy is the Lamb, who was slain,
>> to receive power and wealth and wisdom and strength
>> and honor and glory and praise!"
> Then I heard every creature in heaven and on earth and under the earth and on the sea, and all that is in them, singing:
> "To him who sits on the throne and to the Lamb
>> be praise and honor and glory and power,
>> for ever and ever!"
> The four living creatures said, "Amen," and the elders fell down and worshiped.[7]

Yes, one day we will all proclaim His honor and excellence! I want to be ready, don't you?[8]

Humility Played Out in Real Life

It is not difficult to find examples of pride throughout our society today as well as throughout history, but many examples of humility can also be observed. I'd rather focus on the good examples rather than the bad ones. One particular example of humility is seen in the life of Hudson Taylor. Born in 1832, Hudson grew up in a godly, praying family. Much of his young life he heard his father's fervent prayer for the Chinese people who had never heard of Christ. Hudson decided to go to China as a missionary. Knowing that his frail and sickly body wouldn't hold up very well, he began to exercise and build up his health for the formidable journey. He also studied Chinese, Greek, Hebrew, and Latin and chose to work as an assistant for a doctor so he could learn more about medicine.

Hudson Taylor certainly had that heart of prayer, which, as we said earlier, is a mark of a humble person. One story in particular shows his dependence on God through prayer. The doctor for whom Hudson worked was a bit absentminded and often forgot to pay Hudson on time. Hudson used this as an opportunity to increase his faith and depend upon God to provide for his needs. There were several times when he had no money left. The food ran out, and the rent was due, but God always supplied what he needed. On one occasion, Hudson had only a single small coin with which to buy food when a poor man approached him and asked him to come pray for his wife who was terribly ill. Hudson went with the man, and upon seeing his terrible living conditions with no money for medicine or food, Hudson handed him his last coin, trusting once again that God would take care of his needs. The very next day, Hudson received a pair of gloves as a gift from someone, and inside one of the gloves was a coin worth four times as much as the one he had given away.

Hudson needed this kind of faith as he entered the mission field in China. He would have become discouraged beyond belief if he did not have his faith in a great God. The people of China did not readily accept him because Hudson looked and talked differently than them. He preached the gospel for many months with no results. The missionary society that was supposed to send him money rarely ever did. I wonder if the words of Peter helped him through this time. "God opposes the proud but gives grace to the humble. And God will exalt you in due time, if you humble yourselves under his mighty hand by casting all your cares on him because he cares for you." Hudson kept casting and praying for God's provision. He later said, "Depend on it. God's work, done in God's way, will never lack God's supplies."[9]

Hudson knew that his appearance was distracting to the Chinese people, so he acquired Chinese robes, dyed his hair black, and even attached a pigtail to the back. The Chinese people grew to respect him because he had gone to such an extent to relate to them. Most of the missionaries at that time would not take on the appearance of the people with whom they worked, yet Hudson's actions remind me of what Jesus did in taking on our human likeness. Hudson had a heart for the people of China, and so he gave up his right to dress in what was familiar to him and went the extra mile to reach out to the Chinese through his appearance.

Hudson married an English girl who worked in a mission school there in China. When Hudson became ill, he and his family were forced to return to England for a while. His illness didn't stop him from thinking about the precious Chinese people. While in England he translated the Bible into Chinese, finished getting his medical training, and continued to pray for God to provide more missionaries. God answered his prayers, and eventually the China Inland Mission was started and sent many new missionaries to China.

On one occasion, someone made the comment to Hudson Taylor, "You must sometime be tempted, Mr. Taylor, to be proud because of the wonderful way God has used you. I doubt if any man living has had greater honor." Hudson graciously and humbly replied, "On the contrary, I often think that God must have been looking for someone small enough and weak enough for Him to use, and that He found me." By all means Hudson Taylor had a humble heart filled with gratitude to God for all He had done. Zechariah 4:6 says, "'Not by might nor by power, but by my Spirit,' says the LORD Almighty." We may be weak, but God is strong and can do a powerful work through us.

Another story is told of an eighteen-year-old man who came from a wealthy Chinese family and desired to be trained as a nurse through Hudson's China Inland Mission Hospital. Hsu Chu was eloquently dressed and was the model of Chinese nobility. After a few days of training in the hospital, a superintendent was alerted to a problem with Hsu Chu. When he was asked to clean some muddy boots, Hsu Chu had indignantly refused, saying he was a gentleman and a scholar and did not do such menial tasks. The wise superintendent first took the boots and then cleaned them herself. Hsu Chu sullenly watched her demonstration of humility.

Then she led the young man to her office and asked him to read Jesus' words, found in John 13:14, "Now that I, your Lord and Teacher, have washed your feet, you also should wash one another's feet." His face flushed, and his eyes filled with tears. Hsu Chu put the Bible on his supervisor's desk and said, "May Jesus forgive me. He did menial work, too." From that day forward Hsu Chu joyfully cleaned boots, scrubbed floors, and carried out other menial tasks.[10] Let us all follow the footsteps of Jesus who laid aside His rights and joyfully served others.

═══════ Personal Pursuit ═══════

ADDITIONAL READING: John 13:1-14—Washing the Disciples' Feet.

BASIC TRUTH: True humility means recognizing the greatness of God and looking out for the interests of others.

CHOICES:

- Praise God continually for who He is and what He is able to do in your life.

- Be encouraged by God's presence in your life.

- Be comforted with God's love.

- Be strengthened by fellowship with God's Spirit.

- Be filled with tenderness and compassion toward others.

- Don't put yourself down; instead be busy lifting up others.

- Devote yourself to prayer, casting your cares on Him.

- Live with a grateful heart, sincerely giving thanks to God.

- Think about other's needs and interests, not only your own.

- Have the same attitude Christ had, being willing to give up your rights.

- Serve one another in love and with joy.

- Confess that Jesus Christ is Lord and recognize that His name is exalted above every name.

DELIBERATE PLAN: Caring About Others' Interests and Needs

Is there someone you can reach out to with care or concern right now? We can start with our own family members and then consider the people in our neighborhood and community. How do you show concern and compassion toward someone else? You may want to begin with a card, a call, an email, or a personal visit to show someone you are taking a genuine interest in them. Take a moment to pray and ask the Lord to lead you to a person who needs your care. Sometimes it is hard to know how to help, yet we can ask the Lord to give us wisdom about how to show we care. Then we need to do it. Write in the space below the name of the person you encouraged and how you took intentional steps to care for his or her needs.

I demonstrated care and concern for: _____

_____ .

I showed her (or him) that I cared by: _____

_____

_____

_____ .

Chapter Six

Shine Like Stars in the Universe

*Let your light shine before men, that they may see
your good deeds and praise your Father in heaven.*
—Matthew 5:16

*No Christian is where he ought to be spiritually
until the beauty of the Lord Jesus Christ is
being reproduced in daily Christian life.*
—A.W. Tozer

When circumstances seem bleak, some people seem to shine brightly. In the east Texas town of Tyler, two volleyball teams had the opportunity to demonstrate the beauty of Christian love and humility and became a bright and shining example of what it means to live for Christ. Now, I want you to know that girls' high school volleyball is big stuff here in Texas, and the teams of East Texas Christian Academy and Summit Christian Academy were squared off in a district match. East Texas Christian had been to the playoffs nine times in a row, while the girls from Summit were new to both winning and to the playoffs.

If you have ever watched a volleyball game, you know that diving for the ball is commonplace for most experienced players, so when East Texas senior Morgan Ashbreck (an all-district setter) dove for the ball, it wasn't too surprising. But when she began convulsing and didn't get up, everyone realized something was terribly wrong. With blood pooling on the floor by her head, coaches and assistants immediately came to her aid. Her mom rushed out of the stands and to her side only to hear Morgan whisper to her, "Am I dying?" Fortunately, help quickly arrived, and as Morgan was loaded into the ambulance, her team huddled in the locker room and prayed for their precious friend and team member.

What do you do next if you are the coach? Do you go on playing, putting aside what just happened, or do you forfeit the game and the chance to be district champs? One of the girls said, "Our teammate's in trouble. If she's in trouble, we need to go with her." And so each and every one of them decided to go and be with Morgan, giving up the opportunity to win the championship. As they left the building, the girls walked through the gym and were immediately overwhelmed at the sight of what was happening at the center of the gym. You see, everyone at the game—the families and friends from both teams plus the Summit team—had gathered together in unison to pray for Morgan.

It wasn't about the score anymore; it was about a girl who needed prayer. Actually as soon as Morgan went into convulsions, the girls on the opposing team gathered together on their knees in prayer. Eventually the Summit coach was informed that East Texas had forfeited the game, and it would have been easy to accept the automatic win. No one would have blamed them because this was Summit's first opportunity to shine in the playoffs. But the Summit coach knew her own girls all too well. They refused the forfeit. Instead, she offered a rematch.

At the hospital, Morgan's friends and family began to flood in, filling the waiting room with hugs, tears, and prayers. After a careful examination, it was determined that Morgan had a concussion, and she needed staples to close the wound on the back of her head. Her teammates stuck with her until she left the hospital at 1:00 in the morning with the doctor's assurance she would be fine in the next few days. The only disappointing part was that the doctors told her she couldn't play in the rematch or even go on the long bus ride to the event. Disappointed, but not discouraged, Morgan decided to write a letter to the girls on both teams. At the top of the letter she wrote, "Please make sure the Lady Eagles and the Lady Panthers as well as their fans get this letter. If it could be read to them before the game, that would be great. Thanks."

Here's what she wrote:

> Tuesday night was a changing point in my life, not because it was the varsity volleyball play-offs but because it was a night when God's grace was present and His love filled one small East Texas gym. I cannot express enough how much my coach, Diann Preston, and the Lady Panthers mean to me, in that they would sacrifice an important game so that they could be with me in the hospital. It would not have been wrong of them to continue the game, but I keep hearing over and over, that the game is not what's important. What is important then? I have thought about this over and over and would have to say:
>
> - a team that puts heart before a win
> - an audience that stops immediately and is silent so that a calm spirit could fill the gym
> - two teams that immediately huddle to pray
> - medical aides in the audience who rush to assist or to hold someone's head or hand
> - paramedics who arrive quickly and professionally
> - fans afterwards who form a circle to pray and then rush to support family in the hospital
> - a team who refuses to accept a forfeit
>
> Lady Eagles of Summit Christian Academy, you are on the list of my heroes. I was told your team and coaches huddled to pray, I was told your parents and fans have called to

check on my condition, and I was told that you would not accept a forfeit, rather arranged to continue the game as is, on another day.

So, who will be the real winners tonight? I think the real winners have already been pronounced. One of the teams will win the final game, but both teams are winners in God's eyes and mine.

A paramedic was overheard describing the gym to other medical staff at ETMC. He described a scene of tranquility and peace, a scene of people praying and silently crying, and a scene of parents and staff holding each other's hands, not in rivalry as expected for a play-off game.

Why are people so impressed by this? Because this is not what we are taught as a society how to act. Crush them, kill them…certainly not pray with them, cry with them!

We are taught to go on with the fight. Alison Kirby, a dear friend, said it best in the ER. She said, "Tell them, Morgan, that if they'd allow God back into the schools, then this would be the norm, not the unusual."

So, I'm on a mission to tell people that. If God is present, there will be peace and love. Can two small Christian schools make a difference? They already have. People are curious and questioning, "Why would an undefeated team risk a forfeit, why would an opposing team not accept a play-off forfeit?" The silence is baffling them.

The Lady Panthers are here today to defend a title in my name, to come home winners. I think both teams are already winners because the real fight, which is the fight to die to one's self, has already been won.

In Him,
Morgan[1]

When East Texas and Summit met again, each team gave a valiant effort to win the match. Summit narrowly won and went on to the next round only to lose the championship to McKinney Christian. For the

East Texas girls, it had been a week filled with a variety of emotions. They had watched their teammate being rushed to the hospital, they had received grace from the opposing team, and they endured the loss of their hopes for the championship trophy. It was a tough ending to the season, yet their coach kept it all in perspective. She said, "Our first goal when we started the season was to glorify God. Part of that would be how we treat our teammates and fans and officials. So, when I look back, yeah, we wanted to go far. But we had an awesome season. And Morgan's OK."[2] I think you will agree that the girls who represented both teams shined like stars that season!

Live It Out

It's one thing to learn about the traits of humility—laying down our rights and putting other's interests before our own—but it is another thing to actually do it. The story we just read is a beautiful picture of humility and how when a person practices Christlike humility, they become a bright and shining example to everyone around them. As we continue with Paul's letter, we see he is encouraging this very type of behavior in us. He desires that his fellow believers flesh out what it means to follow Christ. In other words, don't just say you follow Christ; really do it! Here's how he put it:

Therefore, my dear friends, as you have always obeyed—not only in my presence, but now much more in my absence—continue to work out your salvation with fear and trembling, for it is God who works in you to will and to act according to his good purpose.[3]

Now, some may read this passage and be tempted to think that Paul was talking about earning our salvation. Nothing could be further from the truth. In fact, when you look at this passage in the context of the rest of his letter, we read in the very next chapter (chapter 3 of Philippians) about Paul speaking quite harshly and critically toward those who try to say Christians must perform certain works to be made righteous. In our passage today, Paul said to work *out* your salvation, not work *for* your salvation. Obviously he assumed the reader already had salvation through Christ because he called it "your" salvation. So what did he mean by working out your salvation?

Think about it this way. If I were to tell you that I am really into health and physical fitness, you may ask me, "Oh, so what do you do to work out?" If I responded, "Well, I just like going to the gym because it makes me feel fit, but I don't really work out," you would most likely chuckle and walk away thinking, *Yeah right, she's a real fitness nut for sure.* If I am going to say I'm big on fitness, then it needs to be evident in my life. My claim to be fit ought to play out in my actions. In a similar way, it is easy to say I'm a Christian. I may even like to go to church and hang out, but the real question is how my faith plays out during the week. Paul tells us to work out our salvation—to live it out in what we do and say. Our faith in Christ should be continually active, vibrant, and growing.

Pastor and theologian John MacArthur comments about this passage, saying it refers to an "active pursuit of obedience in the process of sanctification."[4] As believers in Christ, our work is an active and ongoing effort to follow Christ and live in obedience to Him. In other words, as recipients of God's grace, we are not supposed to become stagnant in our salvation. We are to be fruitful in obedience and proactive in learning more about Christ and growing closer to Him. As Christians we are not called to complacently live life, but rather we are called to passionately pursue Christ. We are not invited to sit comfortably in an easy chair labeled "Saved" but rather to boldly live lives of humility and loving-kindness toward others.

Careful here! I'm not suggesting that you add more Christian activities or church stuff to your life to be a better, stronger, more important Christian. This passage is encouraging us to continue actively following Christ, not to add more church meetings and responsibilities to our life. Drawing close to Him through personal prayer and getting to know Him through meditating on His Word are how we begin working out our salvation. This is where we fellowship with Christ and learn to walk in obedience to Him. It is easy to think Christianity is all about the outward additions to our life like going to church every

Sunday, attending Bible study, going on a mission trip, singing in the church choir, or serving on the women's ministry leadership team. These things are well and good, but the truth is our faith is stimulated and active when we dwell in the secret place with the Lord and grow in our personal walk with Him.

Interestingly, Paul uses the words "fear and trembling" to tell us how we should work out our salvation. He is not telling us that we should be shaking in our boots as we live under God's mighty hand of judgment, but once again, he is referring to living with humility and with a healthy reverence for God. The opposite of fear and trembling would be arrogance and boasting, which is a common tendency for people who are living the big outward showcase of Christianity. Yet when in humility we draw close to Christ and obey Him, we recognize that it is by His grace that we can do anything good. Herein is an important step in our journey toward humility—realizing that God is working in us not only to do what is good but even to *want* to do what is good! That pretty much knocks out our own prideful attitude when it comes to living and doing things for Christ. Knowing it is God who works in us to both give us the desire and the ability to follow His ways keeps us humble as we depend on Him to carry out His good purpose. We can't take any credit.

God's Good Purpose for You

Do you find it overwhelming to think that God has a good purpose for you? I know I do. In my small perception of God, I naturally assume He is too busy to plan out a good purpose for me. Yet throughout Scripture we are reassured of His plans and purposes. Some people have trouble believing God's purposes are good. They tend to think of God as a cruel taskmaster or a slave driver with a whip, ready to lead us into the most difficult life we can imagine. Paul didn't say that God works in us to will and to act according to His evil plan, His cracked whip, or His never ending demands.

No, God works in us to will and to act according to His *good purpose*. This little phrase can be translated as God's kind intention or good pleasure. God not only knows what is well and good, but He has the intention or resolve to work toward that good. We see this same term used in the first chapter of Ephesians. "He predestined us to adoption as sons through Jesus Christ to Himself, according to the *kind intention* of His will."[5] Again, we find these words used later in the same chapter. "He made known to us the mystery of His will, according to His *kind intention* which He purposed in Him."[6]

Paul wrote in his letter to the Thessalonians, "We constantly pray for you, that our God may count you worthy of his calling, and that by his power he may fulfill every good *purpose* of yours and every act prompted by your faith."[7] I'm also reminded of the well-loved Romans passage, "And we know that in all things God works for the good of those who love him, who have been called according to his purpose."[8]

Do you get the feeling as you read these verses that God has an intentional plan and purpose for us, and it is good? He is calling us to follow Him and to walk with Him because He has a good plan and intentional purpose. He wants us to walk according to His ways, and He wants to help us do it because He has kind intentions for us. He wants us to know the joy of living for Him and humbly walking in obedience to Him. It's funny how so many temptations in this world seem to offer good pleasure, but they leave us less than satisfied. Whether it is living with someone outside of marriage, relying on alcohol or drugs to stimulate pleasure, or coveting more possessions, people search and are often left wanting. But God has a good purpose and a kind intention for our lives, and it is found in Him. No one can take away His good pleasure and kind intention.

Although the Bible tells us that God has good plans for us, it doesn't mean that our life will be nice, sweet, and smooth sailing all the way through. God reminds us that things may be difficult, but He still has kind intentions for us. We see this throughout the lives of the men and women of faith in the Old Testament. Abraham, Joseph, Daniel, and Jonah all faced difficult struggles, but God had a good purpose and a kind intention for them, which played out in a beautiful way in their lives. As His child and a partaker of His grace, He has a kind intention for you as well. Don't be discouraged through the struggles, but rather trust His good purpose for you.

In Jeremiah we read that the prophet was given a message for the Israelites. He told them to get ready because they were going to be captives in Babylon for seventy years. Seventy years! What? That's terrible! Did God really have a kind intention for them? Yes, He did. Here's what Jeremiah told the Israelites. "This is what the LORD says: 'When seventy years are completed for Babylon, I will come to you and fulfill my gracious promise to bring you back to this place. For I know the plans I have for you,' declares the LORD, 'plans to prosper you and not to harm you, plans to give you hope and a future.'"[9]

You've probably heard that verse before, but did you realize it was in the context of the Israelites learning they would be in captivity for 70 years? We are not reassured that all things will be nice and rosy, but we are reassured that God is with us and has wonderful plans for us. As you face challenges and difficulties in your life, you may not be able to understand why something is happening. You may wonder why the Lord allowed this circumstance in your life, but one thing you can do is trust God's kind intention for you. He has a good purpose, and He will equip you with what you need to walk through this difficulty.

When I recognize God has kind intentions for me, I see life from a little different perspective. I know I can trust a God who loves me and has a good plan for my life, even if I don't like what is happening at the moment. Nineteenth century Scottish preacher Alexander MacLaren said, "Seek to cultivate a buoyant, joyous sense of the crowded kindnesses of God in your daily life."[10] Yes, when we have the joyous sense of an overflowing kindness that God has toward us, it changes the way we receive what comes our way. May the Lord's kindness fill our thoughts moment by moment so we can see life with joy and bless others with the type of kindness we have so graciously received!

No Complaining. Really?

If I challenged you to quit complaining and arguing for an entire week, could you do it? What about for a month? Now, that's a little difficult. What if I challenged you to stop complaining and arguing for the rest of your life? Wait! Stop! Don't throw away this book! I'm serious. Let's just take a look at the possibilities here. Paul actually did write to the Philippians and told them to do everything without complaining and arguing, and if we are going to study his letter, we can't throw away the parts we don't like. Perhaps you are thinking, *Aren't there times when we need to stand up for ourselves? Surely God doesn't intend for us to never talk about our difficulties.* Yes, there is a time and a place for sharing our concerns, and we will get to that. Let's take a look at what Paul said and try to gain some insight.

> *Do everything without complaining or arguing, so that you may become blameless and pure, children of God without fault in a crooked and depraved generation, in which you shine like stars in the universe as you hold out the word of life—in order that I may boast on the day of Christ that I did not run or labor for nothing. But even if I am being poured out like a drink offering on the sacrifice and service coming from your faith, I am glad and rejoice with all of you. So you too should be glad and rejoice with me.*[11]

I realize this is a hard saying. I don't like it either! Oh, wait. Does that count as a complaint? Crumb! Anyway, stick with me. Paul is helping us along in our pursuit of Christ, and as we progress, he encourages us to shed some bad habits along the way. Consider this. If we look out for the interests of others, do nothing out of selfish ambition or vain conceit, lay down our rights for the good of others, and actively live out our salvation without pride, then there's simply no room for complaining or arguing. And when we truly believe God loves us and has a good purpose for our lives, then grumbling, whining, and bickering tend to dissipate as well.

Now when I think about complaining and grumbling, I can't help but think about the lovely example the Israelites gave us in the Old Testament. Oh, it's so easy to point to them, isn't it? God miraculously freed them from their chains and brutal slavery in Egypt, led them through the Red Sea, provided their food and water each day, and took them right up to the doors of the promised land. But they fretted and complained. They didn't believe God would do what He said He would do. God told the Israelites that He would bring them into the good land, a land flowing with milk and honey. Sadly, they focused on the size of the people in the land instead of the size of their loving God who created the land and its inhabitants. In Psalms we read a recap of their journey and their grumbling.

> The people refused to enter the pleasant land,
>   for they wouldn't believe his promise to care for them.
> Instead, they grumbled in their tents
>   and refused to obey the LORD.
> Therefore, he solemnly swore
>   that he would kill them in the wilderness,
> that he would scatter their descendants among the nations,
>   exiling them to distant lands.[12]

When we take our eyes off of God's unfailing love and care for us, we can slip quite easily into grumbling and complaining. Our issue is so very important, and it becomes our all-encompassing focus, yet our whining demonstrates a lack of faith in a sovereign God who has a kind intention for our lives. When we grumble and complain, we not only show how little we trust God, but we also introduce worry and anxiety to both ourselves and to those around us. So how do we get rid of our grumbling? Consider the following steps when you are overwhelmed with the need to complain.

1. Turn your eyes upward and thank the Lord for His kind intention for you. One of the greatest antidotes to complaining and whining is to take our focus off of the frustration and look instead to the God who loves us. As we sincerely thank Him for His good purposes and kind intent, we also begin to realize God can take care of our situation, and we don't need to be spouting off about our problems to others.

2. Pray about the situation. Anytime we are about to grumble, we must ask ourselves a simple question—have I prayed about this? Seek His guidance and strength. As you seek God's wisdom on how to handle the situation, also ask Him to help you grow through it. *Lord, what do You want to teach me through these circumstances?* As we pray, we begin to see our worries dwindle. When we bring our challenges to God first, we do not give worry an opportunity to set in. Like wood logs fuel a fire, worry and anxiety fuel complaining and whining. Faith says, "I will trust God's unfailing love through this challenge. I know God can give me the wisdom and direction to see this through."

3. Share your concern if necessary. There are times when we do need to present our point of view or our concern, but we can do it without grumbling or whining. Instead, we can wisely, patiently, and kindly present our thoughts or perspective to the right person but not to all our neighbors, coworkers, and friends. Offer your concerns and be willing to be a part of the solution. Leave the results to God. There have been times in my own life when I eventually realized my way wasn't the best way. Imagine that!

The other night after I spent the day writing this chapter, my husband asked me to do a simple task after dinner. He wanted me to unload several boxes of my books, which had been sitting in the corner of the family room for days, by the way, and place the books on the bookshelf to get the boxes out of the way. Well, I huffed, and I puffed. Didn't he know that I was very busy writing this book and didn't have time for trivial tasks like that? I whined, complained, and told him I would eventually get to it. Then it hit me. I suddenly remembered the topic on which I was writing. At first, of course, I strongly considered just taking the section about complaining out of the chapter. Unfortunately I recognized it wouldn't be right for me as a Christian author to only write about the happy, good parts of the Bible and leave out the tough stuff

I didn't like because I didn't want to unload my books. So I decided to leave this part in the chapter and unload the boxes of books. After I finished unpacking the books—taking all of five minutes to do—I realized an important life lesson. It usually takes less time and energy to do the actual task than to complain about it. Just carry that little nugget with you for a few days and see how it affects your complaining.

To be clear, I am not suggesting that we ignore our feelings. When we get rid of complaining, it doesn't mean we become a Pollyanna and only say nice and happy things. There are times when we must honestly say to friends and family members, "This is hard, and I am struggling." Recently a friend of mine told me her brother was going back for chemotherapy again. He thought the spot on his liver was gone and he was done with chemo, but sadly another spot showed up on his pancreas. His words to his sister were, "I'm not a complainer, but this is really getting hard." There is a difference between complaining and being open with your feelings. We must be open, honest, and real. There are times when we must grieve and be sad. I'm not trying to diminish the importance of those moments.

Complaining is different than sharing your struggles or feelings when you need help or encouragement from a friend. Complaining is a constant dripping of grumbling and whining and telling your troubles over and over again without necessarily trying to find a solution. Complaints usually include the words *always* or *never* in the barrage of disappointments.

- You never help me.
- I always have to take out the trash.
- You always make me do your work.
- I never have the opportunity to have fun.

We must check ourselves and be cautious of these types of grumblings. In the long run, complaining can decrease our faith in our loving God and diminish our efforts to do something positive. So let's consider what is coming out of our mouths. Are we simply sharing our feelings about our challenges in an honest way, or are we repeatedly and faithlessly whining about our situation without praying or looking for possible solutions?

An Argument for No Arguing

What about arguing? Paul didn't just tell us to do everything without complaining, he also mentioned to do everything without arguing. Certainly there are times when we must make a wise petition or request, but like Esther, this can be done with love, patience, and wisdom. And, of course, there are going to be times when we disagree with someone (every spouse knows that), but we don't have to argue, bicker, and become angry. We can have healthy discussions. There are even times when we must agree to disagree. Angry arguments often erupt when we demand to be heard or demand our own way without considering the other person's point of view. What is the key to discussing without arguing? Once again, I believe the answer is praying for wisdom and God's help before bringing attention to a matter. Wait for the right timing, pray for emotional peace, and carefully think through what is and is not necessary to say.

James offers a good solution when it comes to arguments. "Understand this, my dear brothers and sisters: You must all be quick to listen, slow to speak, and slow to get angry. Human anger does not produce the righteousness God desires."[13] When we listen to others first, it has a calming effect on them and on us. Many people just want to be heard, so doing what James says about being quick to listen can dispel a good share of arguments. Take your time, gain your composure, pray before you speak, and, of course, avoid the destructive effects of getting angry. Anger in itself is an emotion common to us all, but in our anger we must not sin by hurting, yelling, or demeaning others.

Paul says there is a beautiful consequence to a life lived without complaining or arguing.

He tells us to stop the grumbling so we may become blameless and pure children of God, without fault in a crooked and depraved generation. He adds that we will shine like stars in the universe as we hold out the word of life. Picture this. What if all Christians stopped complaining and arguing? What if we looked different from the rest of the world because we trusted God rather than grumbling? What if we started wisely interacting with each other instead of angrily bickering with others? The world would be shocked! Then the world may begin to see us as blameless and pure children of God. Our lights would begin shining in the darkness, shining like stars in the universe, beautiful diamonds glorifying and honoring God!

We may have to die to some rights. We may need to think of others' interests as more important than our own. We may need to serve instead of demand our own way. Paul closes this section by mentioning his own suffering, not in a complaining sort of way, but in a joyful way. He says that even if he is poured out as a drink offering, he is glad and rejoices with the Philippians! What? He goes on to say that they too should be glad and rejoice. Now that's a new twist on facing our challenges—be glad and rejoice! Paul saw God's faithfulness and redemption through his suffering way back when he was in the Philippian jail, and now he was seeing it again in the jail in Rome. He could rejoice not because of his difficult circumstances, but because of God's comfort and care through his difficulties.

How do we do everything without complaining or arguing? How do we shine like stars in the world? How do we actively live for Christ? It begins with humility—in the humble, quiet moments alone with Him and in the secret place of prayer, looking to Him who works in us both to will and to act according to His kind intentions for us.

Personal Pursuit

ADDITIONAL READING: 1 Peter 4–5—Living for God

BASIC TRUTH: When we follow Christ and reflect His humility, we shine like stars in the universe.

CHOICES:

- Actively pursue Christ and don't let your Christian walk grow stagnant.

- Remember, it is God who works in us both to desire and to act according to His good purpose.

- Seek God's help to have the ability and the desire to obey Him.

- Pursue Christ, not a bunch of activities.

- Do not allow grumbling and whining to have a place in your life.

- Stay away from angry arguments and don't rudely demand your own way.

- Let your light for Christ shine so that others may see your faith in action and glorify God.

- Rejoice in what God can do even in your difficulties.

DELIBERATE PLAN: Fast from Complaining

To follow Paul's challenge, I want to encourage you to fast from complaining, whining, and grumbling for three days. Write yourself some reminders on sticky notes that say, "No Complaining!" and post them throughout your house in places where you tend to grumble. You may also want to put them in your car and at the office. Actively seek the Lord's help to find your satisfaction and hope in Him. During your fast, I want to encourage you to spend time in God's Word and prayer each morning. Give your cares to God and ask Him to help you guard your mouth and mind from complaining. Ask Him to alert you when you are starting to whine. Warning: The lack of complaints may shock your family, friends, and coworkers, but you will be a happier person, and they will be too! Try it, you'll like it!

CHAPTER SEVEN

$\mathcal{W}$hat Does True Devotion Look Like?

*Be devoted to one another in brotherly love. Honor one
another above yourselves. Never be lacking in zeal, but
keep your spiritual fervor, serving the Lord. Be joyful in
hope, patient in affliction, faithful in prayer. Share with
God's people who are in need. Practice hospitality.*

—ROMANS 12:10-13

*Genuine, living devotion, Philothea (one
who loves God), presupposes love of God, and
hence it is simply true love of God.*

—FRANCIS DE SALES

Who are the heroes in your life? Take a moment to think about the people throughout your life who have inspired you to be a better person or encouraged you to stretch to greater heights. It may be someone you know personally, or it may be a person you read about in a book or magazine or on the Internet. It could be a former teacher or even a family member or friend. Most of us have at least one person we can point to and say, "She was a great example for me. She inspired me to be a better person."

For me, I have had several positive examples in my life. Mrs. Billman, my high school Sunday school teacher, was the picture of a godly women. She knew God's Word, reflected its truths in her own life, and challenged us as students to do the same. Her gentle and wise way of dealing with people and leading us along God's path demonstrated to me what it means to live for Christ and be a follower of His. Her example inspired me to become a teacher. My dad was another powerful example in my life. His enthusiastic and positive way of looking at life's circumstances showed me how to turn my eyes toward hope and not despair no matter what life brings. Dad sincerely cares about others, and as I watch his love in action, I am inspired to reach out and be thoughtful and sensitive toward the people God places in my life.

On a broader scale, women like Amy Carmichael, Corrie ten Boom, Elizabeth Fry, and Joni Eareckson Tada have served as strong role models of women who lived with passion and purpose despite the difficulties they faced. Their stories have touched my life and inspired me in my journey to follow Christ. I can look back over my life and thank the Lord for the people God has used to influence me and develop certain traits within me. The powerful picture of people who live courageously and fearlessly for Christ can serve to ignite a fire in a new generation of believers. It's not necessarily what they say that matters. It's how they live. The heroes in my life exemplify transformed lives. They are sermons in action.

A person's words may influence us, but a person's living example has the power to grip us, inspire us, lead us, and change us. As I was growing up, my dad often quoted a poem by Edgar Guest entitled "Sermons We See." This one line continues to ring in my mind, "The best of all the preachers are the men who live their creeds, for to see good put in action is what everybody needs." The people in our lives can be personally strengthened by the way they see us putting good into action. Our kids learn how to speak kindly and forgive as they watch the way we handle our neighbors. Unbelievers may be drawn to Christ by watching a devoted follower of Christ reach out and genuinely help a person in need. The lady in the checkout line behind us may be encouraged to be more patient when she observes our patient and gentle behavior. A friend may slowly stop gossiping as she recognizes our wise and guarded lips.

People are watching! They are watching our actions and our reactions in various life situations. Remember the story of Paul and Silas in the prison cell at Philippi, which we talked about in chapter one. The other prisoners were intently watching as Paul and Silas responded to the unfair circumstances with prayer and praise. As a result, when their chains fell off, they didn't run, and the Philippian guard came to know Christ. Yes, people are watching how we handle difficulties. They are watching how we react in the midst of unfair situations. They are watching how we respond to frustrations and temptations. Our example may help someone else along life's journey in personal areas such as sexual purity, integrity, hard work, discipline, gentleness, and kindness.

Living by Caring

As we return to our study, we see that Paul caps off his exhortation to the Philippians about humility by telling of two tremendous men who lived their lives according to the principle. Timothy and Epaphroditus looked out for others' interests above their own. Epaphro… who? You probably aren't familiar with him. He didn't write any books of the Bible, and he didn't have any written to him. He was an undercover influencer and an important hero, nonetheless. God used him for important kingdom purposes in the early church, and we will see that he was greatly loved by the believers in Philippi.

It is important to note that the heroes in our lives are not necessarily famous people known throughout the Christian community. God may use one of us as a Sunday school teacher who serves the Lord and demonstrates Christ's love in a rural church in Indiana. God may use one of us as we work in a cubicle at a big corporation to be an example of a faithful follower of Christ to our coworkers. God may use one of us as a nurse, neighbor, or a customer at the dry cleaners. We don't have to be a rock star to make a difference in other people's lives. We just need to be faithful. The true heroes are those who live their lives in a passionate pursuit of God whether they are recognized by the world at large or not.

So Paul highlights Timothy and Epaphroditus, two men whose lives made a difference through their example of following Christ with their whole hearts. Two guys who didn't give up when the going got tough. Two guys who honored and cared for others before thinking about themselves. Paul points to their lives as examples of good in action. He begins with Timothy.

> *I hope in the Lord Jesus to send Timothy to you soon, that I also may be cheered when I receive news about you. I have no one else like him, who takes a genuine interest in your welfare. For everyone looks out for his own interests, not those of Jesus Christ. But you know that Timothy has proved himself, because as a son with his father he has served with me in the work of the gospel. I hope, therefore, to send him as soon as I see how things go with me. And I am confident in the Lord that I myself will come soon.*[1]

We learn several important characteristics about Timothy from this paragraph. Read the passage again and make note of everything you learn about him. Here's my list.

- Timothy is unique. There is no one else like him. The literal translation is "there is no one of equal soul."
- He is unique because he takes a genuine interest in the Philippians' welfare (while everyone else looks out for their own interests).
- He is a selfless servant of Christ.
- Timothy ultimately looks out for the interests of Jesus Christ.
- Timothy has proved himself to the Philippians.
- He is like a son to Paul. At this period of time, Greeks highly valued the service a son gave his father, and so Paul is giving a loving compliment here.

- He has faithfully served with Paul for the work of the gospel.

We can learn more about Timothy from other New Testament passages. In the book of Acts, we find that Paul, while on his first missionary journey, first encountered Timothy in his hometown of Lystra. We also learn in Acts that Timothy's mother was a Jewish believer and his father was a Greek. The Christians in the area spoke highly of Timothy, and that motivated Paul to take Timothy along on his mission even though he had recently rejected another young man by the name of John Mark. Now, here's the biggest demonstration of Timothy's commitment to sharing the gospel—he agreed to be circumcised. He did not want his mixed Greek and Jewish background to cause problems on the missionary journeys. That shows his full commitment![2]

Timothy went on to travel with Paul from town to town, encouraging fellow believers. We learn a few additional facts about Timothy from the letters (1 Timothy and 2 Timothy) Paul sent to him.

- Timothy was young.[3]
- He most likely had a timid personality.[4]
- His mother, Eunice, and grandmother, Lois, taught him about God and helped him grow in his faith.[5]

How beautiful to see the faith both his mother and grandmother passed down to Timothy. If you are a mom or a grandmother, never underestimate the power of your example! Timothy went on to faithfully serve alongside Paul, spreading the message of Jesus Christ. Paul had so much confidence in Timothy that he told him to stay in Ephesus to lead the church there.[6]

Personally, as I look at Timothy, I am reminded that God prepares us for the work we are to do, and He works beyond our weaknesses. No one is the "perfect" example except Christ Himself. We all have flaws, failures, and shortcomings, but God is strong through our weaknesses. Timothy grew to be an influential example to other believers despite his youth and timidity. Timothy wanted to wholeheartedly serve Christ and His people. It meant enduring circumcision, travel, and prison and learning to step out of his comfort zone and genuinely care for others. It meant not thinking about his own image and interests but that of Jesus Christ. Now, there's a powerful example!

Timothy shared the same passionate purpose as Paul—to proclaim the gospel message. His eyes were on Christ and not on himself. He didn't set out to be noted and congratulated as a great example. He simply lived for Christ with all his being. Our goal shouldn't be to grow to be the best example we can be. Our goal ought to be to become more like Christ. To be more like Christ, we must be more *with* Christ. As we spend time with Him—dwelling with Him throughout our day, reading His Word, and abiding with Him in prayer—our lives reflect what it means to follow Christ. His selfless love in us will pour out of us and touch the lives of others.

Honor Men like Him

Epaphroditus offers us another example of becoming more like Christ. Here's what Paul had to say about him.

> *But I think it is necessary to send back to you Epaphroditus, my brother, fellow worker and fellow soldier, who is also your messenger, whom you sent to take care of my needs. For he longs for all of you and is distressed because you heard he was ill. Indeed he was ill, and almost died. But God had mercy on him, and not on him only but also on me, to spare me sorrow upon sorrow. Therefore I am all the more eager to send him, so that when you see him again you may be glad and I may have less anxiety. Welcome him in the Lord with great joy, and honor men like him, because he almost died for the work of Christ, risking his life to make up for the help you could not give me.*[7]

As we can see, Epaphroditus, whose name means "charming," was a blessing to Paul. Consider what we learn about his character in Paul's promo paragraph about him. Here's what I gleaned.

- He was a true brother, meaning a fellow believer.
- He was a fellow worker, helping with Paul's needs as well as serving in the ministry.
- He was a fellow soldier, a cohort in the spiritual battles they faced.
- He was sent by the Philippians to be a messenger and to take care of Paul's needs.
- He felt things deeply. He longed for the Philippians and was distressed when they worried about him.
- He didn't give up easily even when he became ill.
- He risked his life to help Paul and ultimately for the work of Christ.
- Epaphroditus was well loved by the Philippians.
- Paul held him in high regard.

Paul thought so highly of Epaphroditus that he encouraged the Philippians to honor men like him. In other words, Paul was patting him on the back as a great example of who should be honored. We learn later in Paul's letter that Epaphroditus also brought Paul a monetary gift from the Philippians, which tells me he was not only caring and compassionate; he was also trustworthy and honest. It is interesting that we only read about Epaphroditus in the book of Philippians. It is evident to me that he was willing to serve and step out of his comfort zone for the work of Christ. His goal wasn't to earn a big name for himself. His goal was to be used by God in whatever capacity God led him.

God used Epaphroditus to strengthen Paul and bring Paul much needed help from his beloved Philippians. Although he didn't write any books or become some big famous Christian who everyone talks about, he was vital in the work of Christ as he ministered to Paul. I rejoice in the variety of ways God uses us in the body of Christ. Some are the up-front people who are preaching the gospel like Paul, some share in the work of the gospel like Timothy, and some serve as the vital behind-the-scenes people such as Epaphroditus. All are important in the work of Christ. Each has a place of significance in the kingdom.

Devotion Versus Motion

Don't try to be a good example. Did I surprise you a little bit by saying that? Well, I do mean it. Don't set out to try to be some stellar Christian example for others. The reason I say that is because being an example should not be your goal. It wasn't Timothy's goal, nor was it Epaphroditus' goal in life. The truth is both men lived lives that were sold out to Christ, and as a result, their lives became wonderful examples for others to follow. It wasn't their outward actions that made them great. It was their heart for Christ and their deep desire to live passionately for Him no matter what the cost. Their dedication to the work of Christ was born out of their devotion to and love for Christ Himself.

The essence of a devoted life is not about how we look on the outside. It is easy to be deceived by appearances. We may look at someone who fasts seven times a year and think, *Now that person is truly devoted to God.* We may look at another who spends most of their time feeding the homeless and think their devotion to God far outweighs our own. And surely someone who has been to seminary and earned a PhD in theology is sincerely devoted to God. Right? Well, not necessarily. Devotion to God may manifest itself in some of these ways, but we must be careful to label what a devout life really looks like because sometimes the true evidence of a sincere relationship with God happens in the humble quiet place.

Francis de Sales, the sixteenth century priest who later became bishop of Geneva, wrote extensively about the mysteries of the spiritual life. He was gifted in using metaphors and everyday images to portray deeper spiritual truths. As a prolific writer, Francis de Sales' thoughts had a great influence on the church. In one of his works titled *Introduction to the Devout Life,* he wrote about the difference between a truly devoted life in Christ and simply the appearance of such. He begins by referring to a recognized artist of his time and uses his example to illustrate the visual life versus the inner being.

In his pictures Arelius painted all faces after the manner and appearance of the women he loved, and so too everyone paints devotion according to his own passions and fancies. Someone given to fasting thinks himself very devout if he fasts although his heart may be filled with hatred. Much concerned with sobriety, he doesn't care to wet his tongue with wine or even water but won't hesitate to drink deep of his neighbor's blood by detraction and gossip.

Another person thinks himself devout because he daily recites a vast number of prayers, but after saying them he utters the most disagreeable, arrogant, and harmful words at home and among the neighbors. Another gladly takes a coin out of his purse and gives it to the poor, but he cannot extract kindness from his heart to forgive his enemies.

Another forgives his enemies but never pays his creditors unless compelled to do so by the law. All these individuals are usually considered to be devout, but they are by no means such. Saul's servants searched for David in his house but David's wife, Michal, had put a statue on his bed, covering it with David's clothes, and thus led them to think that it was David himself who was lying there sick and sleeping. In the same manner, many persons clothe themselves with certain outward actions connected with holy devotion, and the world believes that they are truly devout and spiritual whereas they are in fact nothing but copies and phantoms of devotion.[8]

After reading de Sales' words, it is tempting to go around trying to judge who has true devotion to God and who does not. We must guard ourselves from judging people's thoughts and motives. Let us instead examine our own lives and consider our own love for God. True devotion is an all-out love relationship with God. It is more than just an intellectual assent or an outward action. It's a love that involves our affections. Paul wrote to the Colossians, "Set your hearts on things above, where Christ is seated at the right hand of God. Set your minds on things above, not on earthly things."[9] As we read in the Old Testament, God commanded the Israelites, "Love the LORD your God with all your heart and with all your soul and with all your strength."[10] Jesus reiterated the importance of this command when He was asked what the greatest command was. He replied, "Love the Lord your God with all your heart and with all your soul and with all your mind."[11]

Devotion to God means loving Him with your whole being—desiring Him above all else, abiding in Him, remaining in Him, and dwelling in Him. All outward signs of devotion flow from the inward reality of a deep love for God. Perhaps you have trouble feeling close to God, and maybe it stems from having a difficult relationship with your earthly father. My friends, as we progress together through the book of Philippians, I hope you are able to see a fresh picture of God. He is a loving heavenly Father who stands with arms wide open, beckoning you to enjoy His warm embrace. Feel His comfort and His grace, which overflow from a perfect love, not a human love. My prayer is that you will experience His sincere love, the love that surpasses knowledge.

She Is a Living Picture

Susie Jennings could have easily given up on trusting God and trusting others when her husband of nine years walked out the door without telling her where he was going. Thirty days later, his body was found in the hills of Oklahoma, hundreds of miles from their home. He had driven there to commit suicide. After a period of grief, Susie knew she couldn't live with anger toward God. Susie would be the first to tell you that she deliberately chose joy instead of bitterness, and she cried out to God to lead her and show her what she was to do with her life. As a full-time nurse working downtown in a large hospital, she drove by homeless people every day. She felt God's nudge to reach out to the homeless she saw on the streets, but Susie ignored the nudge.

To be quite honest, Susie didn't necessarily like the homeless. You see, while Susie was young, growing up in the Philippines, her mom continually invited the homeless into her home to take care of them. They ate her food and seemed to invade her home, and Susie just didn't like them. Now she was feeling God's push to bring them blankets!

The directive from God became so clear in Susie's mind that she collected money from her fellow doctors and nurses, bought a large stack of blankets, and took them to the homeless people she saw on the way to work. She continued to do it and soon became familiar to the homeless people.

One thing led to another, and now Susie organizes the biggest Christmas party for the homeless in the world. Thousands and thousands come from surrounding cities. Homeless families come with their children. Men and women from local shelters and off the streets are bused to the Dallas convention center so they can enjoy a celebration in Jesus' honor. She provides food, shoes, blankets, toiletries, Bibles, haircuts, makeovers, free phone calls, love, and care. Job counseling, housing, education, and other social services are offered to the homeless, and they are even able to reunite the homeless with their families. Thousands of volunteers participate each year. Susie raises funds and donations to provide what can only be described as a gift of love.[12]

Susie Jennings is literally one of the most joyful people I have ever met. She is a prayer warrior who radiates Christ's love and finds joy in serving others. When she doesn't know what to do, she prays. When she doesn't know where donations are going to come from, she prays. When she has trouble with someone, you guessed it, she prays! Susie is sincerely devoted to God, and her trust is in Him. She loves God with all her heart and you can hear it in her words as she speaks about Jesus. More important than her words, we see her devotion to God overflow into her actions of charity and love toward others. Like Timothy and Epaphroditus, Susie shows us what it means to live a life fully engaged in a passionate pursuit of God.

Personal Pursuit

ADDITIONAL READING: 2 Timothy—Paul's Letter of Encouragement to Timothy

Basic Truth: A godly example is the natural overflow of a deep and abiding relationship with Christ.

Choices:

- Love the Lord your God with all your heart, soul, mind, and strength.
- God has equipped each of us with unique gifts and talents.
- Live with wisdom and courage.
- Honor others by serving them.
- Take a genuine interest in the welfare of others.
- Work heartily for the Lord and not for men.
- Be sincerely devoted to God, not just busy with outward actions.
- Ask God to use you to affect someone else's life for Christ.

Deliberate Plan: Say Thank You to a Hero

Take the opportunity to write a note or call someone who has been a positive, loving example to you. It may be that they simply demonstrated God's love and forgiveness, performed some small act of kindness to you, or maybe lived a life of selfless service for the gospel. Whether it was something big or small, take the time to let that person know that their example of following Christ has affected you. Just as Paul encouraged Timothy and Epaphroditus, we all need a word of encouragement now and then to know that we made a difference in someone else's life. By writing your note, you too have taken a genuine interest in another person's welfare and have made a difference in their life by demonstrating Christ's love through the gift of encouragement.

Chapter Eight

*G*etting Rid of Garbage to Gain What Is Priceless

*For my part, I am going to boast about nothing but the
Cross of our Master, Jesus Christ. Because of that Cross, I
have been crucified in relation to the world, set free from
the stifling atmosphere of pleasing others and fitting into
the little patterns that they dictate. Can't you see the central
issue in all this? It is not what you and I do—submit to
circumcision, reject circumcision. It is what God is doing,
and he is creating something totally new, a free life!*
—GALATIANS 6:14-15 MSG

*The most effective poison to lead men to ruin is to boast
in themselves, in their own wisdom and will power.*
—JOHN CALVIN

Lindsay took great pride in clipping and organizing her coupons to
the point that it was almost an obsession. She watched for the
sales and waited for the double coupon days at her local Super Saver
Market. She carefully planned her grocery list according to her budget, making sure she had a few dollars left to buy the sugar cookies

with pink icing and sprinkles as a reward. Lindsay even started a blog to tell others how they could live life on less. Shopping was more than an errand to Lindsay; it was an adventure and a mountain to be conquered!

At the store, Lindsay typically spent a good hour carefully picking out just the right brands to match her coupons. One day after a particularly satisfying shopping victory, she approached the checkout lane with a confident smile, knowing she had saved over $100 on groceries and various sundry items. After the clerk had finished scanning all the items, the unexpected happened. As Lindsay reached toward her overstuffed envelope packed with coupons, the clerk said something that completely toppled her perfect little apple cart. "I'm sorry, but I can't accept your money or your coupons for these groceries." *What?* After all her painstaking work and over-the-top calculations, the store wouldn't take her money or her coupons?

Lindsay felt the heat rising and was about to erupt like Mount Vesuvius when the clerk smiled and calmly said, "Your groceries have already been paid for by the new owner of our store. He wants to build good relations with the customers, so he decided to randomly pick several people in the store today and pay for their groceries. Today is your lucky day!"

You would think Lindsay would have jumped up and down and screamed, "Wahoo! I can't believe it. I've just hit the jackpot!" But, you see, Lindsay's life was wrapped up in watching her pennies and clipping coupons. She had a reputation to maintain with her blog audience. She couldn't have everything just given to her. So right then and there, Lindsay told the clerk, "Thanks but no thanks," and walked out of the store, leaving her hard-earned basket behind. She quickly found another store down the street that would value her coupons and understand the careful planning she put into her shopping experience.

At this point, you are probably thinking, *Well, that is the nuttiest story I have ever heard. That can't be a true story.* And you are right. Yes, I made up the silly story of Lindsay who lives, breathes, and dies for clipping coupons. And, of course, there is no store that I know of that is offering random customers free groceries. I wanted to illustrate how ridiculous it is to refuse a gift just because you worked so hard to earn it. Lindsay missed the gracious store owner's gift because she was so caught up in the value of her coupons and her own hard work. In a similar way, the religious leaders in Paul's day couldn't seem to let go of what they had earned. They were so proud of their accomplishments and the righteousness they had earned by following the law that they couldn't seem to comprehend the true treasure of God's gracious gift through Jesus Christ.

I guess you could say that the Judaizers (Jewish Christians who wrongly believed that it was essential for Gentiles to follow the Old Testament laws) wanted to hold onto their golden coupons in the form of their reputation and righteous acts. They were consumed by what they achieved on their own merit. Their pride blinded them to the fact that God offered salvation through His Son Jesus as a free gift for all who would receive it through faith. We can point a finger at them and think what foolish people those religious leaders were, but then again most of us tend to hold on to certain valuable coupons and think they will get us in good with God. Belonging to a certain church, going on mission trips, memorizing long passages of the Bible, abstaining from alcohol, or teaching Sunday school can all become bragging rights in the Christian community.

These accomplishments are all nice and good, but they won't earn us more of God's love, and they won't pay the price for our salvation. They also don't obligate God to answer prayers exactly the way we want Him to, and they won't guarantee success in this world. Paul makes it quite clear in his letter to the Philippians that these golden coupons of good works are worthless compared to knowing Christ Jesus our Lord. Worthless. Well, crumb! I want my good hard work and righteous coupons to count for something. Now I'm sounding like Lindsay. And we thought she was the silly one!

Watch Out for Those Dogs

As the owner of two mastiffs, we obviously love dogs at our house, but it seems like our current culture is almost over-the-top when it comes to pet adoration. Doggie day spas and specialty boutiques have popped up all over our city. One local boutique is called "Reigning Cats and Dogs." I love that creative title, and I can only imagine every pet who receives something from that store is treated like royalty in their home. Without a doubt, dogs and cats have been elevated to a level of great significance, but it hasn't always been that way. In Paul's day, dogs roamed the streets and were considered filthy scavengers. The term *dog* was used as a derogatory remark by the Jews toward the Gentiles, but Paul used the term to refer to another group of people. Let's take a look at how Paul continues his letter.

> *Finally, my brothers, rejoice in the Lord! It is no trouble for me to write the same things to you again, and it is a safeguard for you.*
>
> *Watch out for those dogs, those men who do evil, those mutilators of the flesh. For it is we who are the circumcision, we who worship by the Spirit of God, who glory in Christ Jesus, and who put no confidence in the flesh—though I myself have reasons for such confidence.*
>
> *If anyone else thinks he has reasons to put confidence in the flesh, I have more: circumcised on the eighth day, of the people of Israel, of the tribe of Benjamin, a Hebrew of Hebrews; in regard to the law, a Pharisee; as for zeal, persecuting the church; as for legalistic righteousness, faultless.*[1]

Notice Paul started off this next section by saying, "Finally," which signifies that he was changing direction from the previous body of the letter. We can observe a difference in his tone as he shifts from elevating Timothy and Epaphroditus as heroes in the faith to warning his fellow believers of certain enemies of the faith. Although he is about to come down hard on the Judaizers, he begins this section with a positive command, "Rejoice in the Lord." The key words here are "in the Lord." He wanted his beloved Philippians to remember that there is great joy in the Lord, not in circumstances, not in accomplishments, and not in people. Our salvation comes from the Lord, and there is joy in finding our hope and satisfaction in Him. Apparently the Philippians needed a little reminder because there were some who were trying to steal the joy of their salvation by making them perform certain works to be saved.

Paul also told them that it was not a problem for him to warn them again—apparently he had previously mentioned this concern. He knew his warning was worth repeating as a safety measure, so they wouldn't be led astray by false doctrines and ideas. Repetition is not a bad thing. There are certain life lessons I can still hear my parents saying to me because they repeated the truths so often, and I'm glad they did. Nagging our husbands is not a good form of repetition, but repeating important truths our kids need to learn can be good when we speak lovingly and wisely.

The warning Paul gave to the Philippians was to watch out for those dogs, those men who do evil. Most theologians agree that he was probably referring to the Judaizers. By calling them dogs and men who do evil, Paul was hitting at the very core of their law-abiding Jewish hearts. They took pride in their squeaky clean righteousness, and they considered themselves far from evil and certainly not on the level of dirty, disgusting dogs.

Spiritual pride was at the core of the Judaizers' motivation. They had built their lives and their reputations on following the law and ceremonial rituals. Surely these golden coupons had to be worth something! The Judaizers just couldn't seem to let go of their dependence on these elements and thought they could earn points toward salvation. It was too much for them to grasp that salvation was a free gift from God, and they could receive it through faith. Instead of seeing good works and acts of righteousness as an overflow from their faith in Christ, they considered these works as a requirement for salvation and demanded that the Gentile believers follow the Jewish law as well.

Circumcision was one of the Judaizers' biggest issues because they couldn't imagine that God would allow uncircumcised people to be a part of His kingdom. Notice Paul didn't even give them the dignity of using the term *circumcision*. Instead, he called them "mutilators of the flesh," which is a term used in reference to pagans and prophets of Baal who mutilated their bodies in frenzied rituals. Paul is clear that circumcision is not a requirement for salvation. As much as the Judaizers wanted to add it to the payment for salvation, Paul stressed it was worthless.

To add insult to injury, Paul began to name the accomplishments he could brag about in his own life. He could boast not only about being an Israelite but also in the highly esteemed tribe of Benjamin. He was also a Pharisee, full of zeal. When it came to legalistic righteousness, he was without fault! If anyone could brag about outward efforts, it was Paul, but he went overboard to make sure everyone understood the outward stuff does not matter to God. It's the inward relationship with Christ that matters. And so we must ask ourselves, *Am I depending on Christ for salvation, or am I depending on outward stuff like the fact that I was born into a Christian family, go to a Christian school, give money to ministries, or live a practically perfect life?*

Outward performance cannot replace inward commitment to Christ. There are a lot of people "playing church" that don't really know Him. We will never be good enough or able to earn what only God can give. Our coupons are worthless in His store. The owner has paid it all. We have been offered freedom from the penalty of sin and the promise of eternal life through the blood of Christ. He has paid our ransom, and our part is simply to receive this gift through faith. True righteousness comes from God

Accounting was never my thing, but I do understand the terms *profit* and *loss*. Paul used these two accounting terms to help us understand the value of our works compared to the value of knowing Christ. Here's how he put it.

> But whatever was to my profit I now consider loss for the sake of Christ. What is more, I consider everything a loss compared to the surpassing greatness of knowing Christ Jesus my Lord, for whose sake I have lost all things. I consider them rubbish, that I may gain Christ and be found in him, not having a righteousness of my own that comes from the law, but that which is through faith in Christ— the righteousness that comes from God and is by faith. I want to know Christ and the power of his resurrection and the fellowship

of sharing in his sufferings, becoming like him in his death, and so,
somehow, to attain to the resurrection from the dead. [2]

As Paul did the accounting of all his life's achievements and credentials, he formed a profit column and a loss column. Now, most of us would want to put all of the great things we have done in our profit column. Being an active member of a church board, visiting a friend in the hospital, sharing Christ with the guy on the bus, helping at the soup kitchen—these are all good things to brag about and count for profit. Paul says he put all those types of good things in his loss column for the sake of Christ. This is quite a defining statement and extremely clear. Paul is not banking on what he has done for his own salvation, it is what Christ has done that counts.

He even takes it one step further when he considers *everything* a loss. He went beyond his credentials and achievements and placed everything in his life in the loss column. The word *everything* would encompass the people he knew, the possessions he had, and the places he had lived. I think he was saying all these things are a loss, and they don't make me who I am. He stripped himself bare of all the possible stuff that gave him significance and, instead, found his significance and salvation in Christ alone. As I write this, I come to the point where I must speculate in my own life and consider what is my "everything"? Am I willing to release everything I tend to find significance in and put them in my loss column? Am I able to say, "It is Christ who gives me value"?

All these golden coupons I've been accumulating over the years by performing good deeds and building my status and reputation don't actually get me in good with God. They don't earn me salvation. They don't earn me more love from God, and they don't satisfy the deep longings of my soul. Trying to find my significance in outward accomplishments and status will only leave me disappointed and frustrated. Christ alone! In Him I live and move and have my being. He does not disappoint. He loves me to the depth of my being, and through Him I am allowed to be called one of God's children and a partaker of His grace. What security there is in knowing my significance comes from Him!

Take My Life and Let It Be

In her short life here on this earth, Frances Havergal experienced her fair share of disappointments, but she also experienced the glorious riches of knowing Christ in a deep and abiding way. Born in England in 1836, Frances lived with what the Victorians referred to as "delicate health." For much of her life, she endured illness and physical pain, yet her spirit was filled with the joy of the Lord, which she expressed through her poetry and hymns. As a gifted songwriter, her words were devotional in nature, drawing believers to a more intimate walk with Christ. Known as the "consecration poet," Frances exemplified the beauty of living for Christ as she reached out to people whenever she saw a spiritual or physical need despite her own disabilities.

The words to one of her most beloved hymns, "Take My Life and Let It Be," demonstrates her dedicated heart for Christ and her motivation for helping others.

> Take my life, and let it be consecrated, Lord, to Thee.
> Take my hands, and let them move at the impulse of Thy love.

Her first book of hymns was published in 1869, but sadly five years later, the publisher went bankrupt, and that put an end to her American publishing career for a while. Although she experienced a loss in income, she was able to say, "'Thy will be done' is not a sigh but only a song!... I have not a fear, or a doubt, or a care, or a shadow upon the sunshine of my heart." Two years later, the offices of her British publisher burned down, taking the only complete copy of her new manuscript called *Songs of Grace and Glory.* She had to start all over again with the words and the music. She wrote to her sisters, "I have thanked Him for it more than I have prayed about it. It is just what He did with me last year, it is another *turned lesson.*" Happily, God granted her the strength, health, and ability to rewrite the work.

When Paul wrote, "I consider everything a loss compared to the surpassing greatness of knowing Christ," I believe Frances understood his heart. It's one thing to know about God, but it's another thing to experience God in such a real way that He gives you meaning, purpose, joy, and strength despite your circumstances. Here's an interesting aside about Frances. According to her sister, "Frances had memorized all of the Gospels and Epistles, as well as Isaiah (her favorite book), the Psalms, the Minor Prophets, and Revelation."[3] Whew! I must say that Frances was a person who loved God with all her heart and passionately pursued Him with her mind, soul, and strength.

"The surpassing greatness of knowing Christ" is a powerful phrase. The Greek word for knowing (*gnosis*), used in Philippians 3:8, actually means to "seek to know," as in an inquiry or investigation. It implies an active pursuit. Paul chose this word because it means "to know someone or something experientially or personally." I think he wanted to encourage his Christian brothers and sisters to move beyond a head knowledge of Jesus and into a close relationship with Him. It's one thing to intellectually know about a person; it's another to spend time with that person, converse with them, and grow close to them.

Paul mentioned a second time in the passage that he wants to know Christ and the power of His resurrection. Me too! Who wouldn't want to experience the kind of power that raises a dead man to life? But Paul didn't stop there; he also wanted to know the fellowship of sharing in Christ's sufferings. Oh! Well, maybe not so much for me on that point. I can easily say yes to knowing the power of Christ's resurrection. Let me get back to you about sharing in His sufferings. I'm embarrassed to admit it, but often my loyalty seems so shallow. I'm guessing you may feel the same way. How did Paul get to the place of wanting to know Christ's power and His sufferings? It's love. It's a love relationship. Wedding vows remind us of this type of love. There we hear the couple vow to love each other "for richer or poorer, in sickness and in health, till death do us part."

True love endures through the good parts and the bad. In his letter to the Ephesians, Paul likened marriage vows to our relationship with Christ when he wrote, "For this reason a man will leave his father and mother and be united to his wife, and the two will become one flesh. This is a profound mystery—but I am talking about Christ and the church."[4] Just as a bride adores her husband and is willing to live through both the good times and the sufferings, so we are to adore our Savior. Paul was willing to endure suffering because he knew and loved Christ. Frances Havergal was able to have joy despite her challenges because her heart was centered on Christ, and she adored Him more than anything else. When Christ is the one we adore, everything else pales in comparison.

The Call

God's call to us has always been to know Him. We read about Jeremiah bringing God's message to the Israelites in the Old Testament.

> This is what the LORD says:
> "Let not the wise man boast of his wisdom
>   or the strong man boast of his strength
>   or the rich man boast of his riches,
> but let him who boasts boast about this:
>   that he understands and knows me,
> that I am the LORD, who exercises kindness,
>   justice and righteousness on earth,
>   for in these I delight,"
> declares the LORD.[5]

Oh, glorious boast! Our boasting should not be based on what we can do but rather that we know the Lord and understand who He is. Do you and I honestly and actively pursue knowing Christ? Not just knowing about Him but really knowing and having a relationship with Him, experiencing His presence in the moment by moment activities of our lives? Prayer is one of the ways we deepen our relationship with the Lord. Prayer is a constant conversation with God and should not be reserved only for meals and church services. Our conversation with God ought to be experienced continually throughout our day. I like how Henri Nouwen refers to this intimacy with the Lord through practicing His presence.

To pray, I think, does not mean to think about God in contrast to thinking about other things, or to spend time with God instead of spending time with other people. Rather, it means to think and live in the presence of God. As soon as we begin to divide our thoughts into thoughts about God and thoughts about people and events, we remove God from our daily life and put it in a pious little niche where we can think pious thoughts and experience pious feelings. Although it is important and even indispensable for the spiritual life to set apart time for God and God alone, prayer can only become unceasing prayer when all our thoughts—beautiful or ugly, high or low, proud or shameful, sorrowful or joyful—can be thought in the presence of God. Thus, converting our unceasing thinking into unceasing prayer moves us from a self-centered monologue to a God-centered dialogue. This requires that we turn all our thoughts into conversation. The main question, therefore, is not so much what we think, but to whom we present our thoughts.[6]

Charles Spurgeon said, "The cure of boasting is to boast in the Lord all the day long."[7] As we think about all the possible accomplishments and achievements we tend to boast about, may we count them as rubbish compared to the surpassing greatness of knowing Christ. As we walk closely with Him in loving prayer, our eyes will turn off of ourselves and on to Him, and our boast will truly be in Him. Oh, to know Him more and understand the enormity of His love! As we close this chapter, I leave you with the prayer Paul prayed for his fellow believers.

I pray that out of his glorious riches he may strengthen you with power through his Spirit in your inner being, so that Christ may dwell in your hearts through faith. And I pray that you, being rooted and established in love, may have power, together with all the saints, to grasp how wide and long and high and deep is the love of Christ, and to know this love that surpasses knowledge—that you may be filled to the measure of all the fullness of God. Now to him who is able to do immeasurably more than all we ask or imagine, according to his power that is at work within us, to him be glory in the church and in Christ Jesus throughout all generations, for ever and ever! Amen.[8]

Personal Pursuit

ADDITIONAL READING: Galatians 3 and 4—Paul's Case for Faith

BASIC TRUTH: To know Christ and walk in a love relationship with Him is life's greatest pursuit.

CHOICES:
- Consider the things you tend to brag about and count them as rubbish.
- Passionately pursue Christ and adore Him above all else.
- Desire to know the power of His resurrection.
- Recognize that knowing Him includes the fellowship of sharing in His sufferings.
- Rejoice in the Lord and not in circumstances.
- Draw close to God through the intimacy of prayer.
- Practice His presence through prayerful thoughts all day long.
- Find your significance in Christ alone.

DELIBERATE PLAN: Boast in the Lord—Get Rid of Rubbish

What do you tend to take pride in as far as your Christian life is concerned? Take a moment to think about it and write down on a piece of paper some of the areas you struggle with regarding Christian coupons and boasting rights. If you are having trouble identifying some areas of pride, just think for a moment about how you would fill in the following blanks.

A strong Christian would never do _____ .

A true Christian should always _____ .

God should be impressed with me and answer my prayers because

I _____ .

Whatever you put in those blanks is probably what you take pride in as a Christian. Now, take the piece of paper with your answers, tear it up, and throw it away. This is a physical way to remind yourself that those things are rubbish compared to knowing Christ. Now take a clean piece of paper or a journal and begin writing the qualities you love and adore about the Lord. Thank Him and praise Him as you write. Practice conversing with Him throughout your day.

CHAPTER NINE

Forget the Past and Press On to What's Ahead

Do you not know that in a race all the runners run, but only one gets the prize? Run in such a way as to get the prize.

—1 CORINTHIANS 9:24

Let us not cease to do the utmost, that we may incessantly go forward in the way of the Lord; and let us not despair because of the smallness of our accomplishments.

—JOHN CALVIN

I sometimes look back and regret that I agreed to do something. Most recently—I'm not sure what got into me—I agreed to run a 5K race with my daughter. Because I was a big runner back in college, you could possibly assume that I would still be a big runner. Well, not so much. Actually I gave up running just after college (twenty-some years ago) because my knees didn't like it anymore. But when my daughter suggested we run in a little race together, I thought to myself, *How hard can it be?*

Let me just tell you how hard it was. Not that I am complaining—

because I gave that up after writing chapter six—but I'm letting you know that as I began to train for the race, my knees hurt, I could barely breathe, and my muscles ached for 24 hours straight. I didn't want to let my daughter down, and so I kept practicing in preparation for the big event. Just before the race started, I encouraged my daughter to go on ahead and run at her own pace and not worry about running with me during the race. She took me up on my gracious offer and zipped on ahead during the first quarter mile. I plodded. Honestly, that's the only way to describe my pace—plodding. Gasping for breath, slow as molasses, I eventually plodded toward the finish line.

It's funny how certain words or phrases come to mind when you are running. The words "press on" kept circling through my mind, especially when I faced the giant hill right before the finish line. Why in the world did they put the finish line at the top of a hill? *Press on,* is all I could think. I had one goal in mind, and that was to press on and cross the finish line. Let's just say I wasn't the picture of physical fitness and agility, and I felt a great sense of relief when my foot stepped over that line. Of course, my daughter was there waiting for me. She had plenty of time to wait for me and had already cooled down and gotten herself something to drink. I'm not so sure I would call the race a victory, but I did learn quite a bit about perseverance and pressing on toward the goal.

Paul used the analogy of a runner in a race to relay a picture of his own personal pursuit to be like Christ. In our last chapter, we read about Paul's deep desire to know Christ, the power of His resurrection, and the fellowship of sharing in His sufferings. Paul counted anything that might bring him pride or glory as rubbish compared to the surpassing greatness of knowing Christ and even becoming like Him in his death. Paul used running as an illustration for persevering to live a Christlike life as we head toward the finish line. He had just finished saying that he wanted to become like Christ in his death and eventually attain to the resurrection from the dead. Then he reassured them that he wasn't ready to obtain the prize of heaven yet. Here's how he put it.

Not that I have already obtained all this, or have already been made perfect, but I press on to take hold of that for which Christ Jesus took hold of me. Brothers, I do not consider myself yet to have taken hold of it. But one thing I do: Forgetting what is behind and straining toward what is ahead, I press on toward the goal to win the prize for which God has called me heavenward in Christ Jesus.[1]

He wasn't in glory yet, but he was headed in that direction. He planned to "press on" toward the finish line. Like my race, the journey may not have been easy, but he had the end goal in mind, and he was going to persevere till the end. He didn't want his past to weigh him down. He looked forward—not backward! His eyes were on the prize when one day he would hear those words, "Well done, good and faithful servant!"

The Race

Because Paul spent much of his ministry in Greece, it is possible he had the chance to see the Olympic Games. Paul used athletic illustrations in much of his writings, making me think he had a major interest in sports. When guys obsess over sports events, maybe it is not so bad, after all. Perhaps they're just imitating the apostle Paul! The Olympic Games were founded in Greece in 776 BC, but many other athletic contests got their start from the Olympic Games. One of them was called the Isthmian Games, which was held in Corinth. When you read passages in the book of Corinthians, you get the feeling Paul had just watched the Isthmian Games.

Do you not know that in a race all the runners run, but only one gets the prize? Run in such a way as to get the prize. Everyone who competes in the games goes into strict training. They do it to get a crown that will not last; but we do it to get a crown that will last forever. Therefore I do not run like a man running aimlessly; I do not fight like a man beating the air. No, I beat my body and make it my slave so that after I have preached to others, I myself will not be disqualified for the prize.[2]

Sporting events and athletic races do offer great illustrations when it comes to life lessons. Discipline and perseverance with a goal in mind are what set a world-class athlete above the rest. Paul applies this same kind of mind-set to the journey of those who follow Christ. We too must press on. The Greek phrase *press on* suggests an intense endeavor. The Greeks originally used the words as a description of a hunter who eagerly pursued his prey. We are to be active in our pursuit of Christ, not complacent. An athlete doesn't become a strong contender by sitting around listening to motivational tapes and studying stories about other great athletes. She must step up to the challenge and step out of her comfort zone, devoted and active in a personal pursuit of her goal.

Looking Forward

Wilma Rudolph could have given up many times the pursuit of her dreams. As the twentieth child of twenty-two kids in her family, she was born in 1940 with polio and also suffered bouts of pneumonia and scarlet fever. Although some said she might never walk, Wilma's loving family worked hard to make sure she received the medical treatment and physical therapy she needed. Wilma started wearing a leg brace when she was five years old. One day at age 11, she decided she had enough of the leg brace, and so she took off the brace and walked down the aisle at church, never to wear it again. When she was 13, Wilma became involved in basketball and track at school. Her running improved to such an extent that she began winning races, and she was invited to a training camp at Tennessee State. There she trained with Ed Temple, who became one of the most influential persons in her life.

In 1956, as a sophomore in high school, Wilma competed in her first Olympic Games in Melbourne, Australia. Although she did not place in her 200 meter competition, her relay team earned the bronze medal. Wilma's persistence and enthusiasm led her to train even harder. She went back to the Olympics in 1960, having already broken a world record in the Olympic trials in the 200 meter. At the Olympics in Rome, she became the first American woman to win three gold medals (100 meter dash, 200 meter dash, and 400 meter relay) and was honored in her hometown's first racially-integrated parade. Wilma went on to receive numerous honors and awards, including the Sullivan Award for amateur U.S. athletes and induction into the Black Sports Hall of Fame, the U.S. Track and Field Hall of Fame, the U.S. Olympic Hall of Fame, and the National Women's Hall of Fame.

Wilma worked her way through college and eventually became a coach and a teacher, but her greatest pride and joy were her four children. Wilma's story has inspired thousands of others to persevere through trials and pursue their dreams. She could have given into discouragement many times, but instead she didn't look back; she looked forward. She pressed on with determination to win the gold. She didn't use her challenges from the past as an excuse to hold her back from achieving her goals.

Often it is our past that plays a big part in our sense of defeat in life. We can become gripped with memories of failures from the past, or we can become stifled by earlier mistakes. Hurts, pains, and disappointments can grow into bitterness, anger, and frustration and serve to keep us on the bench rather than in the game. Paul recognized the importance of letting go of the past and leaning in toward what is ahead. He needed to do it in his own life, not only to forget the regrettable things he had done (like persecuting the church) but also to let go of the pride of the accomplishments he had achieved in the past. Either one would slow him down.

One of the disciplines every sprinter is taught early on in training is to never glance back at competitors during the race. This one simple move can slow her down and cause her to miss out on winning the race. In the same way, we must keep our focus forward and on the goal of knowing Christ and growing in Him. We must relinquish the power that the past holds on us, let go of the past hurts, defeats, embarrassments, mistakes, and even the past accomplishments in which we may tend to wallow. Living with our eyes looking back will only discourage us and trip us up. We are told in Scripture to look back at one thing, and that is the goodness of the Lord and what He has done for us.

Thanking God for His blessings will strengthen us, but rehearsing wounds, mistakes, and miseries will only serve to weaken us. Now, I know it is impossible to erase all the memories from your life. Paul wasn't talking about voiding every memory from your brain. He was basically saying he was no longer affected or influenced by the past. A runner stays focused on where she is going, not where she has been. Whether we are being burdened by regrets of things we did in the past or glorying in things we did in the past, it is time to move forward.

Author and Bible teacher Warren W. Wiersbe put it this way, "Forgetting those things which are behind does not suggest an impossible feat of mental and psychological gymnastics by which we try to erase the sins and mistakes of the past. It simply means that we break the power of the past by living for the future. We cannot change the past, but we can change the meaning of the past. There are things in Paul's past that could have been weights to hold him back, but they became inspirations to speed him ahead. The events did not change, but his understanding of them changed."[3]

God can use the situations in the past to make us wiser and stronger. Let us not allow our past to render us powerless, but rather let us give our past to God and thank Him for the lessons learned. We are to run forward, pressing on to what God has prepared ahead for us. He has a plan for each of us. Don't become entangled in what has happened behind you. Seek God's help in overcoming the grip the past has on your life. In the Old Testament, Lot's wife turned to a pillar of salt. Why? Because she looked back. In the same way, allowing our mind to replay old tapes over and over again can stifle us and rob us of our ability to move forward. We must guard our gaze and concentrate on what God has ahead of us.

One Thing

Can all life's issues be narrowed down to "one thing"? Paul said, "But one thing I do: Forgetting what is behind and straining toward what is ahead, I press on toward the goal to win the prize for which God has called me heavenward in Christ Jesus." There are several other places in the Bible where we see this term *one thing,* and they are similar to Paul's "one thing." I'm reminded of Mary sitting at Jesus' feet while Martha scurried about in the kitchen. When Martha was exasperated and asked Jesus to tell Mary to help her, Jesus answered, "Martha, Martha, you are worried and upset about many things, but only one thing is needed. Mary has chosen what is better, and it will not be taken away from her."[4] What was the one thing Mary had chosen? It was to be with Christ.

David wrote in the Psalms, "One thing I ask of the LORD, this is what I seek: that I may dwell in the house of the LORD all the days of my life, to gaze upon the beauty of the LORD and to seek him in his temple."[5] The one thing David desired was God's presence. When Jesus healed the blind man who was later questioned by authorities, the blind man said, "One thing I do know. I was blind but now I see!" This man didn't understand everything, but he knew one thing. He had met Jesus and experienced God's healing touch, and his life would never be the same. What is your one thing?

Paul narrowed the wide scope of his life down to one thing—pursuing a likeness to Christ. The one thing that propelled him forward was to know Christ and become more like Him. Being conformed to Christ's image was his goal. Although this goal was unattainable on earth, he knew he would one day obtain the prize for which God had called him heavenward in Christ Jesus. Paul wasn't satisfied with staying just as he was and living in complacency as a follower of Christ. He desired to press on with aggressive and energetic action.

Romans 8:29 reminds us, "For those God foreknew he also predestined to be conformed to the likeness of his Son, that he might be the firstborn among many brothers." Becoming more like Christ is not just Paul's calling. It is every believer's calling. Some may point the finger at superhero Christians and say, "Well, that's just their thing. Sure, I am a Christian, but it doesn't consume me." As followers of Christ, our journey doesn't just stop at the point we believe in Him. Trusting Christ is our beginning point of faith, and our journey continues as we seek to be more like Him. Sure, we have different gifts, talents, and abilities. We have different jobs God has given us. No matter what we do vocationally, our calling is to know Christ and become more like Him.

Paul wrote to the Colossians, "Whatever you do, whether in word or deed, do it all in the name of the Lord Jesus, giving thanks to God the Father through him."[6] And then later in the same letter, "Whatever you do, work at it with all your heart, as working for the Lord, not for men, since you know that you will receive an inheritance from the Lord as a reward. It is the Lord Christ you are serving."[7] When we recognize that our higher calling is to be conformed to Christ's image in whatever we do, we find joy in our work because we are working unto Christ and not to men. Our higher calling to become more like Him takes our eyes off of others and puts them on the Lord.

Just as a world-class runner stays focused on the finish line and not on the other runners, so our focus should be on becoming like Christ and not on other believers and how they live their lives. That should certainly reduce comparisons and jealousies, don't you think? Our purpose in life is not about us, what we can achieve, or what other people are achieving. It is about Christ and what He can achieve through us as we surrender to Him. We will never be defeated when our goal is to conform to Him, but we will certainly be discouraged if our life is centered on our own glory or comparing ourselves to others.

Paul wrote with eloquent beauty to the Corinthian church about the transforming work God does in a Christian's life. He referred to Christians as those who have had the veil removed from their eyes so they can see. It was actually a reference to the veil Moses wore to cover his face, which was bright and radiant after meeting with God. The Israelites still had the veil covering their view of Christ. Here is Paul's charge to the Corinthians and also to us, "All of us who have had that veil removed can see and reflect the glory of the Lord. And the Lord—who is the Spirit—makes us more and more like him as we are changed into his glorious image. Therefore, since God in his mercy has given us this new way, we never give up."[8] Notice that he says we are being changed into the Lord's glorious image through the work of God's Spirit, and he said we never give up. It is God's work to transform us, and it is our job to press on to be more like Him.

Overcoming the Past

What kind of future is there for a girl who was orphaned, abused, and told everyday that she was ugly and unlovable? Dorie Van Stone can tell you from her own experience that there is hope in God's love. She proclaims the message worldwide, "There isn't a hurt that God can't heal." Dorie's story started when she was a young girl living in poverty. Her mother couldn't take care of her and her sister, so they were sent off to an orphanage. The women who ran the home were cruel and beat Dorie if she didn't eat all her food or cried or was caught reading when she was supposed to be doing her chores.

Although the seven years in the orphanage were awful, there was one bright spot. A group of college students came and told the kids a Bible story and shared the message about Jesus' redeeming love. God touched Dorie's heart, and she knew that Jesus must be real. She prayed, "They say You love me. Nobody else does. If You want me, You can have me."[9] She instantly knew God's peace and presence. Several weeks after Dorie prayed that prayer, a woman came to work at the orphanage and took Dorie to church on Sundays. She even gave Dorie a New Testament for her thirteenth birthday. This was the first gift Dorie had ever received, and she began to understand more about Jesus.

The orphanage took kids only up to 12 years old, and so Dorie and her sister were moved to a foster family. This is where things went from bad to worse. Dorie was abused physically, sexually, and emotionally in this home. She thought there may be hope when she was moved to another foster home, but the abuse was even worse. Despite the horrible conditions, Dorie clung to the one thing she knew—the love of God and His presence in her life. Finally someone at school reported the bruises, and Dorie was moved to a home where she was cared for and not mistreated. While she was in high school, Dorie lived with a doctor's family. This new family noticed Dorie's talent in drawing and art and encouraged her to go to an art school.

Dorie went on to get a job drawing equipment at an aircraft company. All the while, Dorie's love for the Lord and knowledge of Him continued to grow. One day Dorie heard a missionary speak at her church, and she felt the tug in her heart to be a missionary. She was torn between continuing with a good job and stable income, which she had never known in the past, or choosing a life of missionary work and returning to a situation of having very little in the way of possessions. She decided to enroll in Bible school. It was there that she met and married Lloyd Van Stone. Most women who have experienced a past filled with abuse have trouble sincerely loving and trusting another individual, but God filled Dorie's heart with a love that only comes from Him. They soon became missionaries in New Guinea.

God poured His love through Dorie to the people of New Guinea. Although they were uncivilized filthy people who never bathed, Dorie looked past the outside and saw hearts in need of Christ. Dorie herself had been rejected and ridiculed by the children at school because she arrived filthy and ragged each day, and so God used her own negative past for good as He helped Dorie have compassion for others. When Dorie's own children grew to school age, the mission society required that the children stay at a missionary school several hundred miles away. Her young son had a very difficult time with the distance and separation, so Dorie and Lloyd prayerfully made the decision to leave the mission field.

Just because God changes our circumstances doesn't mean He is finished pouring His message through us. After Dorie and her family returned to the States, she began speaking to church groups and telling others about God's redeeming love. Sharing how God healed the painful emotions and bitterness of her past, Dorie's message was powerful. As her children grew, Dorie traveled around the world, telling people everywhere, "When no one else will love you, God will. He will always be there through thick and thin, good and bad. There is no comfort like His. He loves with a love that will never let you go."[10]

Moving Forward with Fervor for the Future

Paul recognized that as we grow and mature in our knowledge and relationship with Christ, we begin to see trials in a different light. As Dorie matured in the Lord and allowed God to use her past for good, she let go of the power her past held over her, and she pressed on to live for Christ. Ultimately this maturity in the Lord leads us to recognize that there is more to life than this life here on earth. We are pressing on because we know there is a better life ahead. Notice how Paul ends this section of his letter reminding us of our citizenship in heaven.

> *All of us who are mature should take such a view of things. And if on some point you think differently, that too God will make clear to you. Only let us live up to what we have already attained.*
>
> *Join with others in following my example, brothers, and take note of those who live according to the pattern we gave you. For, as I have often told you before and now say again even with tears, many live as enemies of the cross of Christ. Their destiny is destruction, their god is their stomach, and their glory is in their shame. Their mind is on earthly things. But our citizenship is in heaven. And we eagerly await a Savior from there, the Lord Jesus Christ, who, by the power that enables him to bring everything under his control, will transform our lowly bodies so that they will be like his glorious body.*
>
> *Therefore, my brothers, you whom I love and long for, my joy and crown, that is how you should stand firm in the Lord, dear friends!*[11]

How is it possible to press on even through difficulties, pain, and strife? We can press on because we know this is not our final home. We know that one day Christ will transform our lowly bodies so that they will be like His glorious body. This is how we stand firm in the Lord; we look forward to the finish line! Just as Wilma kept her eyes on the gold, so our sights need to be toward our heavenly crown. So, my sister, press on! Right now you may be jogging in life at a delightful pace, or you may be plodding due to pain and difficulties. Keep your eyes on the finish line, knowing that this is not our final home. Press on toward knowing Christ's love and becoming more like Him. Abide in Him. Strengthen yourself in Him. Find your worth in Him.

BE THE BEST "YOU" YOU CAN BE!

Finally, recognize the privilege of being a citizen of heaven. Despite the people Paul referred to as enemies of the cross (apparently referring not only to the Judaizers but to self-indulgent Christians who continued to relish living immoral lives), Paul reminded the Philippians that they were citizens of heaven. In Paul's day, it was the highest privilege and honor to be a Roman citizen. It is interesting to note that citizens of a Roman colony were expected to live up to the standards of citizenship. They were supposed to promote the interests of Rome and live in a way that brought dignity to their city. We too must live in a way that promotes our heavenly citizenship. In other words, live up to the standards of our citizenship, walking in God's ways and living according to His Word.

Paul wasn't the only one pointing to our heavenly citizenship; Peter also talked about the fact that we are strangers in this world because we are citizens of another world. Here's what he wrote to the "aliens" scattered abroad.

> But you are a chosen people, a royal priesthood, a holy nation, a people belonging to God, that you may declare the praises of him who called you out of darkness into his wonderful light. Once you were not a people, but now you are the people of God; once you had not received mercy, but now you have received mercy.
>
> Dear friends, I urge you, as aliens and strangers in the world, to abstain from sinful desires, which war against your soul. Live such good lives among the pagans that, though they accuse you of doing wrong, they may see your good deeds and glorify God on the day he visits us.[12]

As citizens of heaven, we have the responsibility to live godly lives here on earth, and we have the joy of looking forward to our heavenly home. The beautiful truth about our citizenship is that we have a God who loves us and has given us His Spirit to enable us to live a godly life. It is His transforming work that allows us to become more like Him in this life and prepares us for the life to come. Let us set our hearts on things above, where Christ is seated at the right hand of the throne of God!

================= *Personal Pursuit* =================

ADDITIONAL READING: 2 Corinthians 4 and 5—Looking Forward to Our Heavenly Dwelling

BASIC TRUTH: God's Spirit is at work in our lives to transform us into the image of Christ.

CHOICES:
- Consider the *one thing* in life that is most important to you.
- Press on toward knowing Christ and becoming more like Him.
- Do not allow past mistakes, discouragements, hurts, and sins to defeat you.
- Don't wallow or rest in past accomplishments.
- Remember God's goodness, faithfulness, and blessings.
- Persevere through difficult times as He conforms you to His image.
- Ask God to heal the past wounds of your life.
- Live up to the standards of your heavenly citizenship.
- Look forward with joy to your heavenly home.

DELIBERATE PLAN: Releasing the Past

Take some time alone, just you and the Lord. Ask Him to show you if there is anything from your past that is weighing you down as you press on toward becoming like Christ. Is there a past sin, mistake, or hurt you need to relinquish or forgive? Ask the Lord to help you not only identify it but also get rid of it. Cast the care upon the Lord for He cares for you. Seek God's help to stop replaying the past in your mind. Release the power it has over you. Look to God for help and strength to move forward in freedom and forgiveness.

Also consider if you have been resting on past accomplishments or people and have grown complacent in your own growth in the Lord. Renew the commitment to press on toward being more like Christ. Ask God to renew the vigor and fervor you once had when you first came to believe in Him. Do not stay lukewarm in your commitment. Run your race with perseverance, knowing your citizenship is in heaven.

Chapter Ten

Change Your Thinking
and Change Your Life

*Do not conform any longer to the pattern of this
world, but be transformed by the renewing of your
mind. Then you will be able to test and approve what
God's will is—his good, pleasing and perfect will.*

—Romans 12:2

*The secret of living a life of excellence is merely a
matter of thinking thoughts of excellence. Really,
it's a matter of programming our minds with the
kind of information that will set us free.*

—Charles R. Swindoll

He's here! He's here! Epaphroditus is here and he has news from Paul!" Imagine the believers' excitement in Philippi as they gathered to hear the news about Paul. I can just picture the word going out from house to house as the people of the early church put away their work and gathered together to hear what Epaphroditus had to say. Think about their joy as they saw that their friend Epaphroditus was alive, well, and carrying a letter from Paul written specifically to them.

Perhaps they gathered in Lydia's home because in the early days of the Philippians' acquaintance with the gospel, Paul and Silas stayed at her home and conducted meetings there. Surely the Philippian jailer would have been there. Maybe even the slave girl (whom Paul had freed from demon possession) was in the audience as Epaphroditus began to unroll the parchment. The overseers and deacons (bishops and pastors) were probably some of the first to arrive, so they could keep the crowd calm and make sure everyone had a place to sit. How refreshing for this young Philippian church to hear the kind and endearing words Paul used to open his letter, telling them that he longed for all of them with the affection of Christ.

The followers of Christ must have felt strengthened to face trials of their own as Epaphroditus read Paul's proclamation that for him to live was Christ and to die was gain. Certainly they felt challenged when Paul wrote to tell them to be like-minded, humble, and looking out for the interests of others. And I'm guessing that some eyes began shifting around the room when Paul warned them to watch out for those dogs—those Judaizers—who tried to add additional rules to the gospel. Everyone must have felt energized by the words, "I press on toward the goal to win the prize for which God is calling me heavenward in Christ Jesus." Yeah! You go, Paul!

Then the bomb came. All seemed to be going well as Paul challenged and encouraged his fellow Philippians, but then he decided to address two women in particular, and it wasn't a pretty sight. I'm sure Euodia and Syntyche wanted to crawl under their seats when their names were read. They didn't receive accolades like Timothy and Epaphroditus. On the contrary, they were given an admonishment to stop arguing and start agreeing in the Lord. Think about what it must have been like for these two women when the following words were read.

> *I plead with Euodia and I plead with Syntyche to agree with each other in the Lord. Yes, and I ask you, loyal yokefellow, help these women who have contended at my side in the cause of the gospel, along with Clement and the rest of my fellow workers, whose names are in the book of life.*[1]

Ouch! Was it really necessary to mention their names, knowing the letter would be read in front of everyone? I suppose sometimes people need to be called by name, but couldn't he have given them a private note or something? Paul was a pretty intense person, and he was also very deliberate. He obviously thought this situation needed direct attention and was important enough that everyone needed to hear about it and help resolve it. Of course, we do not know the ins and outs of the argument between these two women, but it must have been causing a significant problem if Paul knew about it as far away as Rome and chose to address it openly and boldly.

Aren't you just appalled that these women in the church were disagreeing? Aren't you glad everyone in today's churches gets along so blissfully? Okay, so maybe we too can benefit from Paul's admonishment. It is vital in the body of Christ that we play together well. Outsiders will know we are Christians by our love. Paul was concerned for the unity of the church and the reputation of the believers, and so he pleaded—notice he didn't suggest or ask—with these two women to agree with each other in the Lord. Again, the key words are "in the Lord." When we take our eyes off the issue and put them on the Lord, our perspective looks a little different. We may, at times, need to agree to disagree. We may have disputes or misunderstandings, but we must work toward the goal of agreeing in the Lord, leaving the issue in His care.

Now, there are times when we may feel as though we need to stand up for our rights or what we think is right. We must be gracious and kind as we work through our different viewpoints, keeping Christ in full view. As we learned in chapter five, the chapter on humility, we must sometimes be willing to die to what we want. Christ, the ultimate example of giving up what was rightfully His, can give us strength, wisdom, and kindness as we seek to agree with others in the Lord. Disputes will happen, but we must learn to handle them wisely and appropriately within the body of Christ, always keeping in mind that as believers we ought not to war among ourselves.

Just as all the systems in the human body must work in agreement to function properly, so too the body of Christ must function in unison. Cancer ignores the body's normal function and growth and begins multiplying on its own, warring with the body's healthy system. Pride, jealousy, complaining, and demanding our own way are types of emotional cancers that can destroy a body of believers. Paul was deeply concerned that the cause of Christ and the health of the body of Christ were being destroyed.

Apparently Euodia and Syntyche worked alongside Paul in the cause of the gospel. What would their disagreement do to the young believers they had helped lead to Christ? What would this lack of unity do to the rest of the fellow workers in the Lord?

Paul called on others to jump in and help these women. Think about it. As women observing conflict between two others, what is our natural tendency? Is it to run and help heal the broken relationship and point them back to the Lord? Or do we respond by taking sides, gossiping to the other women of the church, and standing back to watch those in conflict duke it out? Blessed are the peacemakers. We need to work together to encourage love and good deeds between fellow believers and not pave the way for their disagreements. Whether we are in the middle of a conflict that needs to be resolved or are bystanders observing a dispute between fellow sisters in Christ, we must set a common goal to encourage agreement in the Lord.

Peace on the Outside Comes from Peace on the Inside

If you were going to give someone advice on how to resolve conflict in a relationship, what is the first thing you would tell them to do? Off the top of my head, I'd probably say, "Now, ladies, let's hear both sides of the argument. Euodia, you go first. Describe the issue from your perspective and tell us how that made you feel. And then, Synthyche, you tell us your side of the argument."

Well, I suppose you can see now why I don't have my own call-in talk show on the radio! Paul, on the other hand, had the perfect solution. In fact, he packed a powerful one-two-three punch—a peace-filled punch that is—to help the Philippians not only resolve conflict with others but, more importantly, resolve conflict internally. You see, making peace with others begins with experiencing peace in our own hearts and minds. Here's what Paul wrote.

> *Rejoice in the Lord always. I will say it again: Rejoice! Let your gentleness be evident to all. The Lord is near. Do not be anxious about anything, but in everything, by prayer and petition, with thanksgiving, present your requests to God. And the peace of God, which transcends all understanding, will guard your hearts and your minds in Christ Jesus.*[2]

The first peaceful punch comes in the form of choosing to be joyful. Paul had encouraged the Philippians to rejoice in the Lord earlier in his letter, and he repeated it again here with an added emphasis. Be joyful! Choose it! Paul reminded the Philippians that they had a choice about how they handled their circumstances and dealt with the people in their lives. They could choose to be joyful in the Lord, or they could choose to be discouraged, angry, and frustrated in the situation. Paul was a credible source to tell them to rejoice because he was writing this as a prisoner in Rome. If he was at the Waldorf Astoria Hotel in downtown New York, then I would most likely dismiss what he was saying and think it is pretty easy to rejoice when you are living in luxury. But from prison? That's a different story. Joy is not based on perfect circumstances or on perfect people for that matter.

Being joyful in the Lord means delighting in who God is and what He is doing in your life. It's not centered on how people are treating you, what you got for your birthday, or what circumstances you are facing. Joy in the Lord is based on the unchangeable, immeasurable qualities of God, the One who loves us and cares for our hearts. *Rejoicing in the Lord* means dwelling on the high King of heaven who has the power to calm the storm, raise the dead, and feed the five thousand. *Rejoicing in the Lord* means turning our focus to the One who is omnipotent, omniscient, and omnipresent. *Rejoicing in the Lord* means resting in the arms of the Good Shepherd and taking comfort in His love. *Rejoicing in the Lord* means recognizing you are not alone and that the sovereign God of all creation bends His ear to hear your prayers.

Pure joy is knowing that I am a part of God's family and a partaker of His grace. Overwhelming joy in the Lord is knowing that I am completely forgiven. My sin, not in part but the whole, has been nailed to the cross. Over-the-top, overflowing, abundant joy in the Lord is recognizing God's comfort and persevering through difficult times, experiencing His comfort when no one else understands. A river of great joy bubbles up in my heart and overflows within me when I forgive others because I recognize that I have been forgiven of all.

Paul did not intend for us to sit around waiting or hoping to feel joyful. Rejoicing in the Lord is a choice in which we turn our attention and our focus off of our frustrations and on to the Lover of our souls. When we focus our thoughts on who the Lord is and dwell on His great love for us, we cannot help but feel a wonderful delight overwhelm our hearts. Do you see why Paul's first piece of advice about conflict resolution was to rejoice in the Lord? With eyes off of the issue and onto a God who loves you and forgives you, your attitude toward others is bound to change. It's almost impossible to be joyful in the Lord and angry with another person at the same time. Joy and anger don't go together.

Did you notice the word *always* when Paul talked about rejoicing in the Lord? That pretty much covers the good times, bad times, and hard times. Always. Continually rejoice in the Lord no matter where you are or what is happening. Stop right now, put this book down, and take some time to simply reflect on the Lord's goodness and mercy. Thank Him for His blessings. Delight in His excellence and power. Confess your sins and thank Him for His forgiveness. Allow a smile to emerge. I know it's there, and it has been trying to break through to your face for a while.

Evidence of Gentleness

The second piece of peace-filled advice Paul gave to help them work through their disagreement was, "let your gentleness be evident to all." Yes, people are watching. They watch how we handle a frustrating situation with a coworker, a meltdown with an out-of-control toddler, or an inconvenient fender bender. Is our gentleness evident? Gentleness is not a sign of weakness; it is actually a sign of inner strength. Yelling and flying off the handle are signs of weakness and lack of self-control. A strong woman is a gentle woman. In the midst of the frustrations life brings, we can be gentle. We can be gentle when we need to stand up for what is right. Yes, it is even possible to be gentle when we teach, train, and discipline our children. Your gentleness will go much further in solving a problem than rage and anger ever will.

What exactly is gentleness? Gentleness is a fruit of the Spirit of God. The Greek word *epieikes* used here can be translated as "forbearance." It is a type of sweet reasonableness. I like those words! I want to be reasonable, and I want to stand up for what is right when necessary, but I must also have a sweet spirit about it. Take a look at how the same word for gentleness is used in the following passages.

> Remind the believers to submit to the government and its officers. They should be obedient, always ready to do what is good. They must not slander anyone and must avoid quarreling. Instead, they should be gentle and show true humility to everyone.—Titus 3:1-2 NLT

> But the wisdom from above is first of all pure. It is also peace loving, gentle at all times, and willing to yield to others. It is full of mercy and good deeds. It shows no favoritism and is always sincere.—James 3:17 NLT

God is gracious and forgiving to us, and we ought also to be gracious and forgiving to others. God is patient with us and bears with us. May we reflect His goodness in all our interactions. When we are gracious to others and deal with them in humility, we are reflecting the image of Christ. It's easy to be gentle with those who are kind to us, but what about those who disagree with us, make mistakes that affect us, or are unkind to us? Let your gentleness be evident to *all*—not just your nice friends, the coworker who likes you, and your friends at church. To *all!*

Gentleness on the outside comes from a humble recognition on the inside. Along with encouraging us to let our gentleness be evident to all, Paul reminded us "the Lord is near." Does the knowledge of the presence of the Lord change how we speak or deal with other people? It should. Recognizing God's presence in our lives motivates us to honor Him by treating people as He would. He is not standing over us with arms crossed, yelling at us to be gentle. On the contrary, He is lovingly present in our lives, reminding us of His kindness and forbearance toward us as well as giving us the power to reflect His gracious love to others.

Picture a situation in your life when you were maybe not so gentle to someone. Now picture the One who willingly and sacrificially died for you standing by your side, not in anger but as a kind reminder of His gentleness toward all. The Lord is near. Reflect on this truth. Keep it in the forefront of your mind as you deal with people day in and day out. Ask Him, the One who is there with you now, to give you a gentle and gracious spirit as you interact with others. Allow your heart to be filled with gratitude for the patience and forbearance He shows to you every moment of every day. What a powerful and beautiful thought, realizing the Lord is near. He sees what you are going through, He knows your needs, and He is able to give you strength.

Active Casting Makes Conflicts Dwindle

Where do you carry your tension? You know what I'm talking about, that all too familiar feeling that rises up when you have a ridiculous amount of stuff going on or you are stressed or stretched beyond what you think you can handle. For me, I begin to feel the tension as pain in my shoulders and neck. This past Christmas I thought I might have reached my limit. We all know the holidays can be stressful, but add to all that planning my daughter's wedding, writing a book, driving nine hours to Memphis for an unexpected funeral the week before Christmas and then driving back several days later, and hosting both a Christmas eve and a Christmas day dinner at our house. Needless to say, I began to feel that twinge of anxiety course through my body.

When I am stressed, I'm not so nice to be around. The holidays are supposed to be a joyful time, so there is no room for cranky moms. Something had to change. Granted there are a lot of things I need to cut out of my busy agenda, but one thing I didn't want to skip was spending a little time reading God's Word each day. I knew I needed it! I use the reading schedule in the *One Year Bible,* which provides daily readings from the Old Testament, New Testament, and Psalms and Proverbs, to read through the Bible in a year. Here's what I read from the book of Psalms on December 23.

> I cry out to the LORD;
>   I plead for the LORD's mercy.
> I pour out my complaints before him
>   and tell him all my troubles.
> When I am overwhelmed,
>   you alone know the way I should turn.[3]

It was the perfect passage for this poor, pathetically overwhelmed woman! This was just what I needed to read to be reminded that God invites me to turn my troubles, my cares, and my concerns to Him. When I am overwhelmed, my husband, children, or friends may not be able to help me, but God can help me. He can show me where to go, what to do, and what not to do. He can help me see what is worth investing time in and what isn't. Nothing is too small. God wants us to pour out our complaints to Him. I want you to know that very day I did some casting. I cast my cares, my worries, and my anxieties to the Lord and asked Him to give me His peace, wisdom, and joy in return. Do you know what? He did!

The reason I told you that little scenario is that sometimes I tend to forget that God truly does care about my needs. I think Satan would love for all us to forget this fact. When others look at Christians and see us consumed with worry and fear, it sends a message to the world that we don't really believe God cares for our needs. On the other hand, if we cast our cares on the Lord and walk in His peace, we demonstrate to the world that we know our God loves us and cares about us. That's why Paul's words are not just a nice suggestion, they are an instruction. "Do not be anxious about anything, but in everything, by prayer and petition, with thanksgiving, present your requests to God. And the peace of God, which transcends all understanding, will guard your hearts and your minds in Christ Jesus."[4]

When God's peace guards our hearts and minds, we begin to let go of our grip on what we think should happen or could happen. When we trust in God's care for us, we don't angrily try to hold on to what we think is the best solution. And when we rest in the Lord, we don't doggedly fight for our own way. The peace that transcends all understanding keeps us from being worried about something we fear may happen in the future. Do you see that when we place our anxieties in the Lord's care, much of the fodder for our disputes is gone? Many conflicts arise out of fear; fear I won't get what I deserve, fear of what is ahead if we make that move, fear of letting go of the way we have always done it, fear of letting someone examine the truth for themselves, fear of what people will think. Like a caged animal, fear can cause us to lash out at others.

Possibly the most important action we can do to resolve conflict is to give our own personal concerns, fears, and anxieties over to the Lord. Maybe you are afraid to forgive someone. Do it anyway and trust God with your concerns about the results. Perhaps you are afraid to agree with your spouse because you don't know what the future will hold if you go with his decision. Prayerfully cast your concerns to God and trust your future to the One who loves you. Consider the conflicts in your life right now and think about how fear and worry may play a role in those conflicts. Are you willing to give those fears to the Lord? May we be like David who wrote, "I prayed to the LORD, and he answered me. He freed me from all my fears."[5]

I like what Billy Graham had to say. "Happy is the man who has learned the secret of coming to God in daily prayer. Even 15 minutes alone with God every morning before you start the day can change circumstances and remove mountains." Begin each day with a time of rejoicing in the Lord and praising Him for who He is. Confess your sins and thank Him for the gentleness and forbearance He shows toward you. Ask Him to help you be gentle to all. Finally, cast your cares on Him and watch Him move mountains as you see your conflicts dwindle and your hope soar.

What Are You Thinking?

When doctors told Dick and Judy Hoyt that there was little hope for their son, Rick, to live a life like any other child, they took it as a challenge. Due to oxygen deprivation to Rick's brain at the time of birth, he was diagnosed as a spastic quadriplegic with cerebral palsy. Instead of focusing on what Rick couldn't do, Dick and Judy began to look for what he could do. They noticed that although he couldn't walk or talk, Rick seemed quite astute, and his eyes followed them as they walked around the room. They began to teach Rick the alphabet and basic words and tried to broaden his experiences by taking him sledding and swimming.

As they began to recognize Rick's intellectual capabilities and his potential to learn, Dick and Judy knew they needed to find a way to help Rick communicate verbally. An interactive computer was built by a group of engineers at Tufts University for Rick. The computer screen displayed the letters of the alphabet with a cursor that highlighted every letter. Rick was able to move his head against a headpiece attached to his wheelchair to click and select the letters he wanted. His first words of communication at 12 years old were not "Hi, Mom" or "Hi, Dad." They were "Go, Bruins!" The Boston Bruins were in the Stanley Cup finals at that time, and it became obvious from that moment on that Rick loved sports and had been following the games all along.

Aren't you thankful Dick and Judy focused on Rick's potential and not on his disability? But the story doesn't stop there. Rick graduated from high school and then went on to get his degree from Boston University in special education in 1993. A significant part of Rick's story began when he was just 15 years old. He told his dad he wanted to participate in a-five mile benefit run for a lacrosse player who had been paralyzed in an accident. Now, Dick was not a long distance runner, but he agreed to push Rick in his wheelchair in the race. They finished next to last. You and I would maybe become discouraged at this point but not Rick. He told his dad that night, "Dad, when I'm running, it feels like I'm not disabled."

Once he realized his son's perspective on running, Dick never quit. In fact, Team Hoyt has gone on to complete over 1,000 races including marathons, duathlons, and triathlons. They even biked and ran across the United States in 1992, accomplishing a trek of 3,770 miles in 45 days. In the triathlons, Dick pulls Rick in a boat with a bungee cord attached to a vest around his waist. For the biking part of the race, Rick rides in a special two-seater bicycle, and then for the running part of the race, Dick pushes Rick in a custom-made running chair. Once Rick was asked if he could give his father one thing, what would it be. Rick answered, "The thing I'd most like is for my dad to sit in the chair, and I would push him for once."[6]

If you want to see Team Hoyt in action, you can watch several videos about them on www.Tangle.com. If you want to have a good heartfelt cry, watch the one titled "My Redeemer Lives—Team Hoyt." Presented to the tune of "My Redeemer Lives," it shows Dick and Rick doing the Ironman Triathlon together and communicates the sense of victory both feel as they cross the finish line. The video ends with a shot of Rick smiling as he sits at his computer with the screen reading, "I can do all things through Christ who strengthens me." Warning: Watch the video only if you have a tissue or two handy.

Team Hoyt offers us an excellent example of seeing the best in another person. Dick and Judy focused on what Rick was able to accomplish and pursued the activities that gave him hope and meaning. In turn, they found new meaning. You see, not only did Judy and Dick believe in their son's potential, but their son believed in his parents' potential as well. Rick believed his dad was able to stretch himself physically to run a long distance race. The 2009 Boston Marathon was officially Team Hoyt's one thousandth race. Dick will be 70 years old soon, and neither Dick nor Rick are ready to retire!

When it comes to the people in your life, what do you focus on? Do you look at what they can't do, or do you see their potential and focus on what they can do? Paul continued his words of admonishment to the Philippians by telling them to concentrate on what is good in people and life. Here's how he put it.

> *Finally, brothers, whatever is true, whatever is noble, whatever is right, whatever is pure, whatever is lovely, whatever is admirable—if anything is excellent or praiseworthy—think about such things. Whatever you have learned or received or heard from me, or seen in me—put it into practice. And the God of peace will be with you.*[7]

I must admit I can get so tuned in to an annoying trait or difference in someone's personality that it becomes all I see in that person, but when I take Paul's advice and begin looking at what is right and admirable about a person, I see them in a different light. Everyone has excellent and praiseworthy qualities. Sometimes we might need to look a little deeper or with a little more creativity, but I promise the good qualities are there. It's also easy to make assumptions about people's motives. Again Paul tells us to think on whatever is true and lovely. Throw assumptions out the window and focus on what you know to be true. When we change our thinking toward people, we become encouragers rather than discouragers. Peace is built between people who are looking at the best in one another. Disputes and despair result from focusing on the worst in others.

Look at the best in people and your circumstances. What is going on in your life right now? I'm sure you have a few challenges and disappointments as well as some good stuff. I'm guessing there are some things that make you frustrated and angry, but there are also some blessings. I encourage you to do exactly what Paul told the Philippians to do. Think about what is true, noble, right, pure, lovely, admirable, excellent, and praiseworthy. Stop and take a moment to consider the blessings that are happening in your life and get your mind off of the bad stuff. Write down several of the excellent or praiseworthy things that come to mind:

_____

_____

_____

_____

_____

_____

Go one step further and consider the good that can be found in the midst of your challenges. Take some time to think about the lessons you've learned and the growth that takes place when persevering during life's difficult times. If you were to ask the Hoyt family if they have seen good resulting from Rick's disabilities, they would share a long list of blessings. Sometimes it is difficult to see the good in a difficult situation. It may take time to see a redeeming factor grow out of a disappointment, but hang in there. Keep looking. Keep your eyes turned toward hope and ask the question, "What can God do through this difficulty?"

Let's determine to look at each obstacle in life as an opportunity to trust God. Life doesn't have to look so bad. Changing your perspective is a challenge, I know, but it is possible. Begin by concentrating on what is going well in your life (what you previously wrote on the lines provided earlier). Thank the Lord for the admirable and noble circumstances in your life right now. As you consistently thank Him for the good, you will begin to develop an eye for seeing what is true, noble, and right even in the tough stuff. Given any circumstance, most people tend to defer to negative thinking, and so we must determine to retrain our eyes to focus on the pure, lovely, and admirable. Look intently at your blessings, and the size of your dislikes and challenges will diminish.

Personal Pursuit

ADDITIONAL READING: Romans 12—Living Sacrifices

BASIC TRUTH: Your pattern of thinking can help strengthen relationships and open opportunities in your life.

CHOICES:

- Agree in the Lord with fellow believers and resolve conflict graciously and wisely.
- Be a peacemaker for others in conflict.
- Choose to rejoice in the Lord.
- Let your gentleness be evident to all as you recognize the Lord is near.
- Don't be worried or anxious. Instead, experience His peace as you cast your cares on Him.
- Look for others' potential and capabilities. See their best side.
- Concentrate on the blessings in your life even within the challenges.

DELIBERATE PLAN: Practice Paul's Plan for Peace

Do you have any challenging relationships in your life right now? Apply Paul's strategy that he gave to the Philippians. I call it Paul's "one-two-three punch," but it's a punch in a good way. So if you feel like punching someone, try this instead!

1. Rejoice in the Lord always. Take your eyes off of what is so frustrating and turn your eyes toward the Lord. Choose to find your joy in Him and His great love for you. As you concentrate on God's goodness, your attitude toward the people in your life begins to change.

2. Let your gentleness be evident to all. No hateful language, no yelling, no screaming, and no gossiping. Be

gentle in your approach to others because you know the Lord is near.

3. Don't be anxious about anything, but in everything with prayer and petition with thanksgiving, present your requests to God. Before you get upset about an issue or about something that could happen in the future, identify what is making you anxious or fearful. Then pray and cast your cares on God. Don't forget to add thanksgiving! God will give you a peace that passes all understanding. When fear is taken out of conflict, peace begins to take over.

Apply these principles as you seek to agree in the Lord with another person. May God's peace and love transform your conflict into a place of hope and redemption.

CHAPTER ELEVEN

The True Secret to Contentment

God is able to make all grace abound to you, so
that in all things at all times, having all that you
need, you will abound in every good work.

—2 CORINTHIANS 9:8

A contented spirit is a fruit of divine grace.

—GEORGE BARLOW

Did you know that one out of every 20 Americans cannot control their urge to shop? It's true. It's estimated that as many as 17 million Americans are shopaholics, spending to the point of damaging their marriages, their families, and their finances. Unfortunately overspending has become an accepted practice in our productive culture, even in hard economic times. The experts at Bankrate.com say, "In the land of conspicuous consumption, compulsive shopping is the smiled-upon addiction, the butt of countless sitcoms and Sunday comics, one of the few disorders that it's still okay to laugh at."[1]

Why do people overspend? Psychologists have come up with a number of reasons why people have become shopaholics. Reasons range from emotional deprivation in childhood to the need to be in control to the desire to fill an inner void. I would add to their list "lack of contentment." If we are going to be completely open and honest with ourselves, we would have to agree that a restless spirit and a feeling of discontentment are common to most people at some point in their lives. Whether or not we are discontent with ourselves, our spouses (or lack of a spouse), jobs, houses, possessions, or circumstances, we all tend to want something better and desire something more. Our culture actually seems to play against a spirit of contentment. After all, how would the advertising industry survive if we were all completely content?

Contentment doesn't mean complacency. It doesn't mean comfortably sitting back in your easy chair and letting the world pass you by. The Greek term for contentment is connected with the concept of sufficiency or satisfaction. A person who is content experiences a heartfelt satisfaction, a God-given peace, and a joy in life that is not based on people or circumstances. The opposite of contentment is restlessness, grumbling, unhappiness, and a never-ending search for fulfillment. This may seem like a bold statement, but ultimately I believe at the inner core of discontentment is a lack of trust in God and a disregard for His great love for us.

What's So Great About Contentment?

My dog Bentley must be the most discontent creature in the world. If she is inside, she wants out, and if she is outside, she is scratching to come back into the house. While I've been writing this paragraph, I've let her in and out three times. She's a precious gentle giant, but she really doesn't know what she wants, and she is driving me crazy. Where's the Dog Whisperer when you need him? Discontentment is not a pretty sight in dogs or in people. It is not an endearing quality for anyone.

Paul was a doer, a go-getter, a dynamo, and a never-stay-in-one-place type of guy, but he was a content man as well. He wrote about his ability to be content in any situation when he penned his letter from prison to the Philippians. I like what he had to say here. I even encouraged my daughters to memorize part of this passage when they were in their early teens and we were about to go on a long family vacation. "I have learned to be content whatever the circumstances" is a phrase for every teenager to memorize, don't you agree? Well, I guess it wouldn't hurt every adult to memorize it too. Here's the whole passage.

> *I rejoice greatly in the Lord that at last you have renewed your concern for me. Indeed, you have been concerned, but you had no opportunity to show it. I am not saying this because I am in need, for I have learned to be content whatever the circumstances. I know what it is to be in need, and I know what it is to have plenty.*[2]

He was content even when he was in need? How can that be? If I am in need, doesn't it follow that I would naturally be discontent? We must ask ourselves, is it the things I have that make me content, or can I have a content heart even when I have needs? The life changing lesson we learn from Paul in this passage is that contentment, like humility, is a heart issue. We may have external needs, but we can still have a content heart and generally peaceful attitude toward life.

There are many examples of people who do not have an abundance of possessions but are rich in joy and contentment. One particular example I observed stands out clearly in my mind. Several years ago our family drove to an underprivileged area in Dallas to deliver turkey dinners to several families who had helped with a Christian after-school program. We weren't even supplying the turkey dinners; we were just using our SUV to help deliver them. Our job was to go to the door, take the turkey dinner inside, sing a few Christmas carols (which was pretty scary because we were not a musical family), pray with the family, and leave.

As we entered the quite meager homes, we were received with amazingly kind and joyful smiles. Each of the families graciously welcomed us into their home. Typically the scenario went like this. We sang our pitiful repertoire of two Christmas songs to the family (who graciously smiled and listened), chatted with the family members for a short while, and then usually someone from the family would offer to pray. Their prayers were deeply felt and full of gratitude. From what I can remember, each of the families prayed something similar to this: *Oh, wonderful, glorious, heavenly Father, thank You for Your many blessings. We are grateful beyond measure for all You have done for us. We are happy in You. You have given us everything we need, and most importantly You have given us salvation through Your Son, Jesus. We can never thank You enough for Your love for and kindness to us, dear Lord. Thank You also for these dear people and this turkey dinner that they have brought us. I pray that You would bless these kind folks and help them to have a good Christmas.*

Whoa! What a prayer! How beautiful and gracious! I'm telling you honestly each home was consistent with the next—their prayers overflowed with joy, thankfulness, and contentment. Mind you, they all lived in simple dwellings with very few possessions, yet they were the picture of contentment in the Lord, satisfied in Him. As our family piled back into our SUV and returned to discontented North Dallas, we had learned a valuable lesson. Contentment is not based on what you have or the neighborhood in which you live. Contentment is an issue of the heart. It is recognizing God's love and being grateful for His care. Some of the most discontent people I know are the wealthiest people I know. It is true that there are discontent people in every strata of society and in every country. You can go to an impoverished culture in Africa and find content people, and you can also find discontent people in the same circumstances. It's a choice of attitude.

We see this concept of contentment throughout the New Testament. In Paul's first letter to Timothy, we read, "But godliness with contentment is great gain. For we brought nothing into the world, and we can take nothing out of it. But if we have food and clothing, we will be content with that."[3] I like that attitude! I like to be around people with that kind of attitude. I'm afraid to look in the mirror and consider how I fall short of that very attitude.

Oh, Lord, open my eyes to my own selfish desires when trying to find fulfillment in possessions or people. Oh, Lord, thank You for providing for my needs. Flood my heart with Your peace and the joy that comes from being satisfied with Your love.

The writer of Hebrews reminds us, "Keep your lives free from the love of money and be content with what you have, because God has said, 'Never will I leave you; never will I forsake you.' So we say with confidence, 'The Lord is my helper; I will not be afraid. What can man do to me?'"[4] Because we know the Lord is our helper, followers of Christ can look different from the rest of the world, and we don't need to be afraid. We can have confidence in knowing that we are not alone. God will never forsake us. Confidence in the Lord as our helper is at the very root of contentment. Do you really believe He is your helper? Is your confidence built on the sure foundation of God's goodness to you?

David had this type of God-confidence and satisfaction. I'm assuming you may be slightly familiar with Psalm 23, which I believe is one of the greatest statements of contentment ever uttered. "The LORD is my shepherd; I have all that I need." The twenty-third Psalm begins with a powerful statement of trust and confidence in the Lord, and you can sense the theme of contentment throughout this poetic work. Let's read the psalm together, and as we do, underline every phrase that hints at having our needs met by our good Shepherd.

> The LORD is my shepherd;
> > I have all that I need.
> He lets me rest in green meadows;
> > he leads me beside peaceful streams.
> > He renews my strength.
> He guides me along right paths,
> > bringing honor to his name.
> Even when I walk
> > through the darkest valley,
> I will not be afraid,
> > for you are close beside me.
> Your rod and your staff
> > protect and comfort me.
> You prepare a feast for me
> > in the presence of my enemies.

> You honor me by anointing my head with oil.
> My cup overflows with blessings.
> Surely your goodness and unfailing love will pursue me
>   all the days of my life,
> and I will live in the house of the LORD
>   Forever.[5]

He makes contentment in the Lord seem so beautiful and poetic, doesn't he. Contentment develops in our life as we place our trust in the Shepherd's care. I'm actually not sure how someone who doesn't know the Lord achieves contentment. On the other hand, I'm not sure how someone who sincerely trusts the Lord can be discontent. When we consider our great God, the One who loves us and knows what is best for us, we can put our confidence in His providential care. Whether we are going through lean times or times of plenty, we can remain satisfied in the sufficiency of God. Even when we don't understand why we are going through a certain issue, we can trust in His care.

Like a sheep that is dependent on the care of its shepherd, are you willing to place your desires in God's hands and trust in His love for you? We may not understand why He doesn't make our life just as we want it to be, but we can trust His loving care for us. As a good shepherd who lovingly cares for his own, God tenderly helps us, holds us, and leads us in the way we should go. With our eyes on Him, right now let us say out loud together, "I have everything I need!" Did you do it? Did you say it out loud? It feels good, doesn't it. If you are in a coffee shop right now, I bet the people around you think you are slightly crazy. Oh well! Just sit there with a smile of contentment on your face; it will drive them nuts.

The Secret

Several years ago a book hit the bestsellers list titled *The Secret*. The author, Rhonda Byrne, claimed she had discovered the ancient secret to getting what you want in life. Her beliefs were based on a mixture of religious and philosophical ideas. At the opposite end of the spectrum, we read that Paul has found "the secret," but it wasn't the secret that Byrne proclaims in her book. Paul's concept was quite different

(margin note: Just Enough)

indeed! Instead of finding the secret to selfishly getting everything you want, Paul's secret was based on being content whether you have what you want or not.

Here's what he wrote to the Philippians.

> *I have learned the secret of being content in any and every situation, whether well fed or hungry, whether living in plenty or in want. I can do everything through him who gives me strength.*[6]

How about that for a secret? Imagine being content in every situation because Christ gives you strength! You've most likely heard the phrase, "I can do all things through Christ who strengthens me." And you've probably heard it applied to everything under the sun, but Paul did not write this phrase to inspire you to climb the corporate ladder, go bungee jumping, buy a giant house, or take up a new hobby. If we keep this phrase in context, we understand he was talking about the strength to be content. Not that any of those achievements I mentioned are wrong, I'm just saying that the phrase "I can do all things" has often been misconstrued. I've seen the "I can do" statement overused and abused in way too many self-help, positive thinking, motivational type books and messages.

The truth is Christ can give us the power to be strong when we struggle with dissatisfaction or discontentment. He can strengthen us when we find ourselves in a situation where we feel as if we can't go on. Our good Shepherd can hold us and help us when we find ourselves in need.

Paul said he had learned to be content whether he had plenty or was in need. Do we really need to learn to be content when we have plenty? Maybe we do. Oddly, it can also be a challenge to be content when we have a lot of money and stuff available. Let me give you a food example (my favorite kind of example). Picture an all-you-can-eat buffet. When you have a marvelous display of food in front of you, do you say to yourself, "I'll only take what I need"? No. If you're like me, you'll take what you *want* plus more! Yes, it's hard to limit ourselves and be satisfied and content when there is plenty available to us.

An extremely wealthy friend of mine told me one time, "It is hard to raise content kids in a wealthy home because they can always have more. You never have the excuse of, 'No, you can't have that because we can't afford it.' There are no clear boundaries as to when to stop buying and declare it is enough." I actually never thought about the challenges of being content from that point of view. Perhaps you are wishing you had the opportunity to find out what it is like to have that kind of challenge with contentment! The point is that no matter if you are well-off or if you struggle to make ends meet, Christ can be your anchor, giving contentment no matter what the circumstances.

There are a variety of situations in life where we may struggle to have a content spirit. In these particular times, we have a choice to try to make it through on our own or turn our eyes toward the Lord and seek His strength in the midst of our uncertainty or unwanted circumstances. We can choose to move toward contentment or contempt. We can live with a peace-filled trust and dependence on God, or we can live with anger and resentment toward Him and our situation.

What about the 38-year-old single woman? Can she be content without a spouse? *I can do everything through Christ who gives me strength.*

What about the 18-year-old who feels as if she is the only believer in her school? *I can do everything through Him who gives me strength.*

What about the wife whose husband just lost his job? *I can do everything through Him who gives me strength.*

What about the young Christian mother who just found out her child is severely autistic? *I can do everything through Him who gives me strength.*

What about the parents who had high hopes for their child, and now he is an addict? *I can do everything through Him who gives me strength.*

What about the woman who can't seem to stop eating. *I can do everything through Him who gives me strength.*

Whether it is a difficult job, an insensitive husband, or a desire to keep up with your neighbors, Christ can give you the strength and wisdom to be content. Paul pursued Christ first, and contentment was produced in his life as a result.

A Practical Path to Contentment

Are you dissatisfied or feeling unhappy or discontented in an area of your life right now? Are you restless or desiring more love, attention, or a thing? It is important to do a little self-evaluation at times to consider if there are any areas in which you need to seek Christ's strength. Reread Psalm 23 and spend some quiet time simply reflecting on the words, "The LORD is my shepherd; I have all that I need." As you reflect on this phrase, ask the Lord to show you any areas of discontentment you need to give over to Him. Consider areas in life where you find yourself angry, unhappy, or wanting more.

Now, let's be realistic; not all dissatisfaction is bad. There are times when our lack of satisfaction can lead us to do something positive. For instance, if a person is overweight and continues to live an unhealthy lifestyle, her dissatisfaction over her weight may lead her to eat healthier foods and exercise. A frustration about clutter may lead a person to take positive steps to reorganize her home. One example of dissatisfaction turning into something positive is actually near and dear to my heart. My daughter Grace, as a student at Baylor University, felt frustrated when she observed the rising level of poverty in Waco, and so she began reaching out to the kids in Waco. She started an art program called Waco Arts Initiative, which gives kids a positive environment to learn art and an uplifting place to go to after school. Waco Arts Initiative is making a difference in the lives of the impoverished kids in Waco. Certainly dissatisfaction can lead us to do something positive.

Contentment doesn't mean staying put and never stepping out. Look at Paul who pressed on and dynamically pursued the spreading of the gospel. If you are feeling frustrated in a certain area, I encourage you to lay it before the Lord and seek His guidance. Allow Him to lead you along a new path or to a greener pasture. I am saying all of this in the context of obeying His Word. For instance, finding a greener pasture does not apply to a marriage in which you are feeling dissatisfied. First and foremost, as we pursue Christ, we must walk in obedience to Him.

Christ can give us the strength to be content in our lives' not-so-perfect scenarios. As we consider the areas in which we do not feel content, I want to lead you down a practical path of finding your strength in Him. Here are several steps to lead you down the road to a place called *contentment.*

Step One: Praise and Thank the Lord

Yes, praise Him in the midst of your discontentment. Praise Him for being your Father, your rock, and your refuge. Praise Him for the power and strength only He can give. Praise Him for His sovereignty. Praise Him for the fact that He is not surprised by anything, and He makes no mistakes. Turn your eyes toward your Provider and praise Him for His care. As you do, you will begin to take your eyes off of what you want and place your focus on the Giver of all good gifts.

As I mentioned before, the opposite of grumbling is gratitude. Instead of remaining in the land of discontent, discover the joy of thanking God even for the times of need and especially for the times of plenty. When we sincerely thank the Lord for the blessings in our lives, we move out of frustration and begin to embrace where we are. We begin to see that blessings can be found even in the worst of circumstances. Did you notice in the last chapter that Paul included the instruction to be thankful in the middle of your worries and concerns? "Do not be anxious about anything, but in everything, by prayer and petition, *with thanksgiving,* present your requests to God. And the peace of God, which transcends all understanding, will guard your hearts and your minds in Christ Jesus." He also wrote to the Thessalonians, "Be joyful always; pray continually; give *thanks* in all circumstances, for this is God's will for you in Christ Jesus."[7]

Step Two: Confess and Turn from Sin

[handwritten annotations: TRUST & OBEY! TRUST HIS SOVEREIGN WILL — THE "BIG PICTURE"]

Sin is so dissatisfying! You are never further away from contentment than when you are in the middle of sin. The irony is we think sin will make us happy and content, and yet it does just the opposite. Sin always lets us down. It is unfulfilling, deceptive, and enticing. Ultimately our strength to be content comes from God, but if we are running away from God by living in sin, we end up a long way from contentment.

Step Three: Ask for God's Strength and Wisdom

God invites us to seek Him and bring our requests to Him. He wants us to find our strength in Him and go to Him for wisdom. When we ask God for help, we are taking an active step in trusting Him and not ourselves. Ask Him to give you a new perspective in your situation. Ask Him to give you His perspective. Remember, trust in the Lord with all your heart and lean not on your own understanding. In all your ways acknowledge Him, and He will direct your paths.

Step Four: Choose to Embrace God's Plan

Instead of trying to fix things so life will be perfectly smooth, consider what God wants to teach you in the midst of your challenges. Trust His love and care for you. Now, I'm not saying that we shouldn't try to improve ourselves or seek out the best in our circumstances, but I am saying there are situations that can't or won't change, and we must learn to embrace them. Instead of always trying to find satisfaction somewhere else, we must come to a point of enjoying God's care for us right where we are.

Step Five: Share Your Struggle

Cultivate a friendship with someone who desires to pursue Christ like you do. Ask her to pray that you would lean on God's strength in your area of discontent. Pray for each other and encourage each other in the Lord. Get together on a regular basis to ask each other how it's going in the area of contentment. When we face our discontentment and share it with a friend, it helps us move from recognition to victory. In the book of James, we read, "Therefore confess your sins to each other and pray for each other so that you may be healed. The prayer of a righteous man is powerful and effective."[8]

Lana and Brett were experiencing a difficult time with their son who has severe learning difficulties and discipline issues. Lana admitted that she wanted things to change. She wanted God to fix her son, and she struggled with why God would allow this challenge in their lives. One day at church, everyone in the congregation was told to thank the Lord for the gifts God had given them. Lana asked God to lead her to what she should thank Him for, and she felt as though God was directing her to thank Him for the struggles with her son. She argued with the Lord because she surely didn't think of these challenges as a gift from Him.

Right then and there, her heart began to change as God reminded her that He makes no mistakes and that her son's struggles were a gift from Him. Lana had never looked at her situation as a gift from God's loving hands. She immediately changed her focus from being angry and discontent with her situation to embracing it as a gift from God. This new perspective literally revolutionized the way she dealt with her son and family. Her changed attitude and content spirit permeated her life ever since. When we change our perspective and begin to see God's sovereignty in the picture of our lives, we grow to be content women.

A content spirit is a reflection of our trust in God's loving care for us. We may not understand why things turn out the way they do, but we can know that God loves us and will be with us to strengthen us through the difficulties. We bring honor to Him when we live with the satisfaction of knowing He cares for our needs. Discontentment and restlessness only lead to frustration and bitterness and show the world we don't really trust in the care of our Father.

Oh, Lord, thank You for Your presence in our lives. Give us peace in our hearts—a peace that passes all understanding—as we embrace the place where You have brought us. Lord, help us to see Your kind provision and give us the strength to be content in any and every situation. May our lives reflect our delight in You! You are the good Shepherd, and we have all that we need.

Personal Pursuit

ADDITIONAL READING: 1 Timothy 6:3-21—Godliness with Contentment Is Great Gain

BASIC TRUTH: The secret to being content is finding our strength in Christ.

CHOICES:

- Be content in any and every situation.
- Remember contentment is a heart issue and not based on what you have.
- Trust God's love for you and remember He is your good Shepherd.
- Praise the Lord for being your provider.
- Be thankful in all circumstances.
- Confess and turn from sin.
- Examine the areas of dissatisfaction in your life and seek God's strength.
- Find a fellow encourager to help you in your journey toward contentment.

DELIBERATE PLAN: Memorize Psalm 23

You can do it! Often we look at memorizing a passage as dreadful and challenging. I want you to look at memorizing Psalm 23 as a powerful and positive step toward contentment. Could we have a greater reminder than this poetic passage? You will find that the comforting words of this psalm come back to you throughout your day especially when you are tempted to become worried or restless because of difficulties. Psalm 23 is a constant reminder that your Shepherd lovingly cares for you. Here are a few tips on memorizing:

1. Write the verses on index cards and carry them with you.

2. Practice whenever you are in the car, waiting in line, doing the laundry, washing dishes, or vacuuming. Review your verses before you go to sleep at night.

3. If you work out, go over the verses while you are exercising. The rhythm and the extra oxygen to the brain seem to help.

4. Draw silly pictures to help you remember the words. Our brains can remember silly pictures better than a list of words. For instance draw a stick figure of a shepherd making you lay down on green pastures and then leading you by quiet waters (a river with the word *shhh* or a "No Talking" sign beside it).

5. Say the verse aloud to someone you know. Try to use it in conversation with a family member or a friend.

CHAPTER TWELVE

Be the Blessing
in Your World

*Be imitators of God, therefore, as dearly loved children and
live a life of love, just as Christ loved us and gave himself
up for us as a fragrant offering and sacrifice to God.*
—EPHESIANS 5:1-2

*When God's work is done in God's way for God's
glory, it will not lack for God's supply.*
—HUDSON TAYLOR

Imagine a young bride packing up five trunks filled with her lovely
wedding gifts and setting sail with her new husband across the
Pacific Ocean to serve as missionaries. In 1930, Darlene and Russell
Deibler started their newlywed life together, making their first home
in a bamboo hut as they brought the gospel message to the tribe of
Kapaukus who lived on the island of New Guinea. Darlene had an
instant rapport with the natives, but unfortunately their work with
the precious people of the island was short lived. As World War II
spread across the Pacific, the Japanese army invaded New Guinea, and
the Deiblers were forced to move to a nearby island. They worked at a

Bible school with other missionaries on the island, but soon it became too dangerous to stay there, and all the missionaries in the area had to escape to the nearby mountains.

Leaving most of their possessions behind (yes, sadly all of those wedding gifts), they continued to live in their mountain hideout. The Japanese army eventually found them and took Russell and the rest of the men to a prison camp. One elderly man, Dr. Jaffrey, was allowed to stay with the women, living in the mountains for a year. Dr. Jaffrey's unwavering faith helped strengthen Darlene during this time. She grew to respect Dr. Jaffrey as a father and was grateful for the comfort and wisdom God provided through him.

Eventually they were all taken to a Japanese prison camp where they lived in harsh conditions. The guards treated the women cruelly and forced them to work long hours with very little to eat. After Dr. Jaffrey was moved to another camp, Darlene despaired, wondering how much more could be taken from her, and yet she learned to depend on the Lord for her comfort and care. God used Darlene to bring the women in her barracks together as a close-knit group. She led them in Bible reading and prayer, giving strength to their weary souls. God graciously allowed Darlene to find favor with the commander as he observed how she was respected and loved by the prisoners. I'm reminded of the story of Joseph in the Old Testament. He was unfairly imprisoned in Egypt, yet God allowed him to find favor with the authorities, and he was appointed overseer of the prisoners. In a similar way, the prison commander put Darlene in charge of the building in which she and the other women dwelt.

One day the news reached Darlene that Russell had died in his prison camp, yet because of Darlene's godly influence in the camp, even the Japanese commander of the camp offered her condolences and tried to comfort her. Darlene, with her eyes on the Lord, was able to tell the commander that she had hope in Jesus and shared the gospel message with him. The commander himself was brought to tears. How ironic that the one trying to give comfort and dry her tears now had tears of his own.

Unfortunately Darlene's troubles weren't over yet. The secret police accused Darlene of being a spy, and she was taken off to a horrible prison where she was beaten and only allowed to eat one cup of rice each day. She became so weak and ill that her hair actually turned white despite being a young woman in her twenties! It's hard to imagine how she must have felt when she was given the death sentence, but God wasn't finished with her. He had important plans for her. Just in the nick of time, the commander of her old camp was able to convince the secret police officials that she was innocent. In a dramatic moment that mimics an action-packed motion picture, several officers drove up and stopped the execution just as the guards were drawing their swords. Phew!

They took her back to her old camp, and you would think things would have been fairly uneventful as she returned to the camp and her position as manager of all the prisoners. Not so. The bombings forced the women to sleep in ditches at night. Their barracks were burned, making it necessary to live in little makeshift huts in the jungle with very little food. By God's grace she was able to survive until Japan finally surrendered. Darlene had spent three years in confinement and weighed a meager 80 pounds by the end of the whole ordeal. When she was finally able to board a ship to head home, she thought to herself that she never wanted to come back to these islands again. Think about it. She lost her health, her husband, her possessions—everything—and she was only 28 years old. But as she saw the Christian natives running to the shore to say good-bye to her, her hardened heart began to melt.

Darlene came home to the States and eventually remarried a wonderful man, Jerry Rose. She passed away in February of 2004, having lived a full life and sharing the gospel message everywhere she went. She wrote a book about her experiences titled *Evidence Not Seen* (Harper Collins, 1990). In a very real sense, Darlene knew God was her provider even in the darkest times. She also knew what it meant to be a living sacrifice, allowing God to use her no matter what the circumstances. Despair was transformed into hope, and weakness was replaced by God's strength. She gave her all, and God held her, comforted her, and provided for her.

God's Precious Care

In my opinion Darlene is a hero. She lived for Christ and found her help in Him. She brought countless others to Him through the example of her own faith and hope. I'm inspired by her life of blessing and her trust in the God who cared for her needs. I want you to read what she wrote about an experience that happened to her just after she found out Russell had passed away. Here are her words.

There is nothing that will plunge a person into despair more quickly than to suppose what could happen. This was another example of the worries of tomorrow that never come, robbing us of the joys of today. Poignant sadness, overwhelming me for the hurt of others, released the tears from my own widowhood. I was alone and I had time to weep, but with the tears came healing. In my moment of terrible aloneness and sorrow for a world of people so devastated by war, I heard someone with a beautiful, clear voice singing the song "Precious Name, Oh, How Sweet" outside my cell, but he was singing in Indonesian, "Precious is Your name, a shelter that is secure!" My heart burst with bright hope! The "time to weep" was past; it was a "time to laugh."

"O Lord," I cried, "forgive me. It isn't a game of 'suppose.' I live in the sure knowledge that 'the name of the Lord is a strong tower: the righteous runneth into it, and is safe.' The name of Jesus, Your precious name, is my strong tower of defense against the enemy of despair. It is my shelter that is secure; I enter in and am safe."

But who was the singer? How could he know I needed that song at that moment? Of course he couldn't know, but he loved God, that is sure. I had to see him. I scrambled up to the transom. My eyes probed the late afternoon light—no one by my door, no one in the courtyard other than the guard and night watchman. They were talking, and I knew they were totally unaware of the singing! Listening to this hymn of hope and assurance coming from I knew not where, great awe filled my heart. Quietly I slipped to the floor and bathed my soul in the presence of my God.

Darlene added this note. "When I shared this with the late Dr. A.W. Tozer—the modern-day mystic, as he was called—he said, 'Girl, did you ever think that God could have sent an angel?' Yes, Dr. Tozer, indeed I did."[1]

Isn't it wonderful to be in a place of God's precious care? Darlene knew firsthand what it was like for God to supply all of her needs. I wonder if, in those darkest hours as she experienced grief, beatings, and hunger, she may have reflected upon Paul's words as he faced similar challenges. Paul had often been beaten and had very little on which to survive, yet he leaned on God to meet his needs in any and every situation. God used the Philippians to help meet some of Paul's physical needs. On the flip side, God used Paul to help meet the Philippians' spiritual needs. The poverty of the soul is one of man's most dire conditions, and how blessed are those who bring spiritual nourishment to the hungry of heart. Think about how God used Darlene to offer the food of God's Word to the women in that prison camp. He used her to meet the spiritual needs of those women as well as the commander, whose life was changed forever.

When Darlene had nothing else to give—no money, no food, no possessions—she was left with only one thing. She had God's Word to strengthen the people He placed in her life. Just as Dr. Jaffrey poured it into her life, she in turn poured it into the lives of others. What has God given you? How does He want you to be a blessing to others? As we consider Paul's closing words to the Philippians, let us think about the fragrant offering we can give to others. Paul begins by letting the Philippians know how grateful he was for their help, especially when others didn't offer it.

Here's his thank-you note of sorts.

Yet it was good of you to share in my troubles. Moreover, as you Philippians know, in the early days of your acquaintance with the gospel, when I set out from Macedonia, not one church shared with me in the matter of giving and receiving, except you only; for even when I was in Thessalonica, you sent me aid again and again when I was in need. Not that I am looking for a gift, but I am looking for what may be credited to your account. I have received full payment and even more; I am amply supplied, now that I have received from Epaphroditus the gifts you sent. They are a fragrant offering, an acceptable sacrifice, pleasing to God. And my God will meet all your needs according to his glorious riches in Christ Jesus.[2]

The Philippians gave. They gave gifts whether it was money or food or clothing or all three. We don't know exactly what it was, but we do know their gifts were helpful to Paul while he was in prison. The Philippians even sent Epaphroditus as a messenger to care for Paul's needs. Paul felt amply supplied by their generous help, and they didn't just help him out once. Paul wrote that they sent aid again and again. He also pointed out that, sadly, other churches did not share in the matter of giving. They didn't choose to participate in the opportunity to be a blessing to Paul. Perhaps they were too busy or didn't recognize Paul's needs while in prison. Perhaps they just didn't care or value Paul enough to give. Whatever the reason, all I can say is, boy, did they miss out on being a part of something that was way bigger than themselves!

When we sacrificially give to others, the recipients are not the only ones who benefit. As we generously give, we too have the joy of meeting others' needs, furthering the gospel through ministry, and bringing compassion to people in need around the world. There is a great satisfaction in knowing we have played a part in helping others. Certainly we must give wisely and prayerfully, but as we do, we have the opportunity to be a part of something bigger than ourselves. Think about the excitement the Philippians must have felt by helping Paul take the gospel far and wide. How sad for the people who chose not to participate.

A Fragrant Offering

Are you a fragrant aroma, or do you stink? It's a simple question and not a bad one to ask ourselves on a regular basis. In other words, am I a blessing to those around me, or am I a discouragement to the people in my life? Do I honor God by lifting up and sincerely loving others? Or do I live for myself, trying to get what I want from other people? Am I a lovely flower, bringing beauty to this world through my words and actions, or am I an unpleasant drain, sucking the life right out of people by complaining and putting them down? Do I give generously of what I have to help the needs of others, or do I hoard what I have because I never know when I'll need it? I'm going to go out on a limb here and guess that you want to be a fragrant aroma to others.

The term *fragrant offering* that Paul used in his letter referred to a thank offering. In the Old Testament, God instructed His people to give an offering as an expression of thanksgiving to the Lord. As Christians we no longer offer the Old Testament type of sacrifices, a fact for which I am extremely grateful. But that doesn't mean we do not offer spiritual sacrifices. In his letter to the Romans, Paul wrote, "I urge you, brothers, in view of God's mercy, to offer your bodies as living sacrifices, holy and pleasing to God—this is your spiritual act of worship."[3] The writer of Hebrews challenged believers in the same way. "Through Jesus, therefore, let us continually offer to God a sacrifice of praise—the fruit of lips that confess his name. And do not forget to do good and to share with others, for with such sacrifices God is pleased."[4]

A sacrifice is an act of worship. It is an offering to God that pours forth from a grateful and humble heart. More than that, it is an offering that costs us in some way. It may be obvious, but I'll state it anyway—a sacrifice is typically an action or a thing that is not easy for us to give. The ultimate picture of sacrifice is what Christ did for us on the cross, suffering and dying on our behalf. It was the purest example of love.

God calls us to be "living sacrifices," offering what we have as instruments to be used by Him to bring glory to Him. Paul said the Philippians' gifts were a fragrant offering, an acceptable sacrifice, pleasing to God. When I think of acceptable sacrifices compared to not-so-acceptable sacrifices, I can't help but be reminded of Cain and Abel. Cain offered up what was easy. It was simply the fruit from his garden, but God required a blood sacrifice, one that came with a price. More important than the sacrifice was the heart of the one who offered it. Cain didn't seem to be interested in what pleased God; he wanted to offer what was easy for himself.

Sadly, often our giving is not so different than Cain's. It's easy to give from our excess money or time, but it's much more challenging to stretch ourselves in the area of giving. We should be wise and prudent with our time, budget, and talents, but we must also live with generous and sacrificial attitudes in these areas. It may mean that we need to give beyond what is easy and convenient. Acceptable sacrifices are not necessarily comfy ones. Living generously and sacrificially is difficult, but it brings great joy and blessing as well. Here's what it could mean in practical terms.

- Take a dinner to a sick friend even though she lives on the other side of town.
- Open your home to an acquaintance who needs a place to stay.
- Be nice to the girl no one else will talk to.
- Don't tell the juicy story about someone else during the lull in the conversation.
- Give up your lunch to help someone in need.
- Take the time to write a letter to a soldier, prisoner, or someone needing encouragement.
- Give more than just your tithe to help someone in ministry.
- Do something kind for the person who was unkind to you.
- Sincerely pray for your enemies.
- Lift up someone else with your smile even when you don't feel like it.
- Speak kindly to someone you don't think deserves your kindness.

- Lend to someone without expecting anything in return.

Sacrificial living and giving mean that we give our best and not our halfhearted leftovers. We must recognize that as we are giving to others, we are really giving to the Lord. In Malachi we read about the Israelite priests being admonished (or perhaps we should say scolded) for offering shoddy, pitiful, blemished sacrifices. They offered the worst to God when God required the best. The priests were going cheap on God. I guess they thought God wouldn't see or wouldn't care. Silly people! They forgot who God is. They failed to remember God's holiness and that He is the God who sees all. I'm so glad we never forget that, right? Anyway, here's what God told the priests in the book of Malachi.

> "A son honors his father, and a servant his master. If I am a father, where is the honor due me? If I am a master, where is the respect due me?" says the LORD Almighty. "It is you, O priests, who show contempt for my name.
>
> "But you ask, 'How have we shown contempt for your name?'
>
> "You place defiled food on my altar."…."Cursed is the cheat who has an acceptable male in his flock and vows to give it, but then sacrifices a blemished animal to the Lord. For I am a great king," says the LORD Almighty, "and my name is to be feared among the nations."[5]

Well now! I'd say God was a little less than pleased with the Israelites throwing away sacrifices. May we offer acceptable sacrifices through our giving of our time, talents, and treasures. Let's stop giving God our little pitiful leftovers. Paul told the Colossians, "Whatever you do, work at it with all your heart, as working for the Lord, not for men, since you know that you will receive an inheritance from the Lord as a reward. It is the Lord Christ you are serving."[6] Now, here's a warning to any of my dear precious readers who love to go on guilt trips. Don't push yourself into a legalistic "I've got to perform for God" type of mentality. The perfect sacrifice has already been paid for our sins in the form of Jesus Christ. We cannot earn God's favor any more than Christ already has on the cross. He is the perfect, unblemished Lamb that takes away the sin of the world. Our spiritual sacrifices are acts of worship to God. Let us honor Him with good gifts and fragrant offerings, not haphazard stinky ones.

I do want to point out one last thing that Paul said. Along with telling the Philippians that their gifts were fragrant offerings and acceptable sacrifices, he added that they were pleasing to God. Sacrifices were only "pleasing to God" if they were offered with a correct attitude. As we live generously and sacrificially, let us also live gratefully. Anytime we are giving of ourselves, we can choose to have a grateful attitude.

Thank You, Lord, for all You have given me. I offer this gift of my time to Your service. Thank You, Lord, for the financial blessings You have given to me. I want to worship You by giving back. Thank You, Lord, for the talent You have given me. I willingly offer it to be used for Your glory.

We experience true joy when our attitude of giving is in the right place. If our attitude is concerned about what we will get in return, we are headed for disappointment. If we are serving to bring glory to ourselves, then we will be left with nothing more than an empty feeling inside. If we are doing something just to please others, we will most likely become frustrated. Let's be 100 percent transparent here. It is rare that we ever give or do for others out of completely pure motives. That being said, we can still have a right attitude about serving, sacrificing, and giving. It all comes down to choosing to be thankful and turning our eyes upward to worship and praise God through our giving. As we do, our focus shifts, and our attitude changes. We become cheerful in our giving, and as we know, God loves a cheerful giver!

What's in Your Hands?

Lynn has multiple sclerosis, a chronic, often disabling disease that attacks the central nervous system. In a physical sense, Lynn has to depend on the help of others. But Lynn is not a burden, she is a blessing. Her sweet spirit ministers to everyone she is around, including her family, her friends, and her acquaintances; pretty much everyone with whom she comes in contact. Lynn may not be running around bringing dinners to others—although she was the queen of serving and giving before her diagnosis—but Lynn is a fragrant offering. She gives what she can in the way of kindness, encouragement, and a good word to others.

We all have something to give. A young boy gave his lunch of five loaves and two fish. Mary gave her alabaster jar of perfume to anoint Jesus' feet. The widow gave her mite. Lydia gave her home. Epaphroditus gave his time, his heart, and his care. The Philippians gave generous gifts. Paul gave up his freedom, his profession, and his position as a Pharisee so that he could give his time and talents to proclaim the gospel of Christ. Each of us has something to offer to the work of God's kingdom. Each of us can be a blessing to others. What do you have in your hands? What has God equipped you to do? We all have something to offer.

The folks at Disability Resources Incorporated in Abilene, Texas, have something to give. DRI is a wonderful place for adults with physical and mental disabilities. It not only has a loving home environment but also vocational opportunities. The special folks at DRI have learned how to make soaps, lotions, chocolates, and sauces that they sell all over the country. The staff helps them discover what they can do, not worrying about what they can't do. They even started a handbell choir, allowing the folks to give the gift of music to audiences. Recently I had the opportunity to see and hear the handbell choir perform and was moved to tears by the music from these lovely people.

As I watched them perform, I was reminded of the variety of ways God has equipped us to give. We all have something to give. The folks at DRI discovered what they could do and how they could give it to others. God has equipped each of us with gifts and talents—no matter how small—to share with the people of this world. We should never say, "But I don't have anything to offer." Allow God to use you in whatever way He has equipped you. Reach out to others with what you have.

The beauty of being a blessing is that you receive a blessing. You don't go out looking for it, but it typically comes back to you in some form or fashion. When you serve others who are in need, there is truly a euphoric feeling that follows. When you show mercy, you receive mercy. Remember Jesus' words, "Give, and it will be given to you. A good measure, pressed down, shaken together and running over, will be poured into your lap. For with the measure you use, it will be measured to you."[7] Jesus wasn't talking about money there. He was talking about acts of love, kindness, and forgiveness.

Paul offers a beautiful reminder to his Philippian friends. He tells them that God will meet all of their needs according to His glorious riches. Bible teacher Warren W. Wiersbe commented, "God has not promised to supply all our *greeds*. When the child of God is in the will of God, serving for the glory of God, then he will have every need met."[8] God's glorious riches are unfathomable. He is Lord of all. The Bible reminds us that God is able to do "immeasurably more than all we ask or imagine."[9] If you have ever felt inadequate, unable, underequipped, or overwhelmed when it comes to being a blessing to others, let me reassure you that God will give you what you need.

Has fear held you back from using your gifts and abilities to be a blessing to others? Be strengthened by Paul's words, "God will meet all your needs according to his glorious riches." Perhaps you are struggling with forgiveness, thinking you just can't do it. God will meet your need according to His glorious riches. And by the way, He is overly, abundantly wealthy when it comes to forgiveness. Maybe you are having trouble being a blessing to someone who is emotionally needy and annoying. Ask God to give you wisdom to set wise boundaries, but also ask God to give you a genuine love for that person so that you can be a fragrant aroma. Just as a pleasant scent can overcome a bad smell, so our gift of love can bring beauty to a difficult person.

God will equip you with what you need to be a blessing to others. Don't be afraid. Don't hold back. Look to Him to give you what you need to be a gift to the people He places in your life. Remember, you don't need to meet every need, but you can do something to bring joy to another person. Ask the Lord to lead you and guide you to where you should give and help others. It may not be in ministry; it may be that God leads you to reach out to the neighbor next door, the person working in the nearby cubicle, or the student who seems lonely at your school. No one is useless. Everyone has something to offer this world. Be the blessing!

Personal Pursuit

ADDITIONAL READING: 1 Corinthians 12–13—Gifts and Giving Them with Love

BASIC TRUTH: God has equipped you to be a blessing to the people around you.

CHOICES:

- No matter what your circumstances, you have something to offer this world.
- Be a fragrant aroma and not an awful stench.
- Ask God to give you what you need to be a blessing.
- There are a myriad of ways to give to the people God places in our life.
- Giving is an act of worship.
- Giving often requires sacrifice.
- Give your best; not your leftovers.
- Give with a grateful attitude.
- Trust God to meet your needs as you step up and step out to be a blessing to others.

DELIBERATE PLAN: Scent Evaluation

Every now and then, we need to reconsider how we are affecting the community around us. We can read a chapter like this and sometimes fail to think about specific ways the truth therein relates to our own life (although it's always easy to think about how it relates to others). Prayerfully interact with the truth from this chapter and think about what kind of aroma you give off to family, friends, neighbors, waiters, people in your church, people in garden club, book club, or quilting circle, and so forth. Ask yourself the following questions. If you are really brave, I would encourage you to ask someone close to you to give you their evaluation of you as well. Ouch! Perhaps that is a little scary and painful, but it can also be helpful and eventually joyful. Here are the questions:

- In what ways am I a precious blessing to the people around me?

- In what ways am I a stench to others because of my negative attitude?

- What changes do I need to make to be more of a fragrant aroma and less of a stinker?

- Am I generously and joyfully giving myself, my gifts, and my talents to others?

Now that you have done a little scent-evaluation, consider where you are going to actively step forward to be that fragrant aroma.

The Passionate Life

> *For in him we live and move and have our being.*
> —ACTS 17:28

> *Faith is a living, restless thing. It cannot be inoperative.*
> —MARTIN LUTHER

When my daughter decided she wanted to go to Texas A&M University, we weren't too thrilled. As Baylor University alumni, my husband and I didn't have fond memories of the Aggies because they are diehard fans with over-the-top traditions. We thought to ourselves, *Who would want to go to a school where no matter the setting they let out a loud "whoop" every time their school name is mentioned—even in a church service?* We slowly warmed up to the idea. Well, I warmed up to it immediately when I took my daughter to the orientation at the school, but it still took Curt a semester and a half to be okay with an Aggie in the family. Now, I must admit that through the years, we have both grown to love the school and are very impressed with the caliber of students we have met from there.

One thing you should know about the school is that the students don't just attend school at Texas A&M; they experience a life transformation.

Most of the students, my daughter included, attend Fish Camp before their first year of school begins. They enter the camp slightly anxious and full of anticipation, and they return from Fish Camp completely changed into an all-out Aggie. There's no looking back. They live, breathe, and die with the traditions of Texas A&M. Their blood turns maroon and white, and they have an immediate bond and connectedness with other Aggies throughout the ages, which we outsiders will never understand. Aggies live with a life-changing passion.

What would a life lived with a Christ-centered passion look like? The apostle Paul gave us an example in his own life, and he also gave us inspiration and instruction through his letter to the Philippians. "Knowing Christ" was Paul's ultimate theme—not just knowing about Him, but truly living, breathing, and dying with Christ as the center of his being. There was no mistaking which school Paul represented. His zeal for Christ played out in his words and actions every step of the way.

Recently my friend Karyn gave me a book called *Fresh Start* by Doug Fields. The reason Karyn gave me this book was because we do a weekly webtv show together called "Fresh Start,"[1] and she thought it was funny to read a book with the same title. One section in the book especially caught my eye. It is entitled "Determine to Live with Passion." Here's what the author had to say about the topic.

> Passion goes deeper than excitement. I can get excited about a Diet Coke and a hot dog at a ball game. Excitement comes and goes. But passion bubbles up from our souls. It's what we live for most. It's what gets us up in the morning and keeps us going strong each day...
>
> To gain passion, we must both choose it and pray that God will develop it within us. I like to say that passion "wakes up" as we yield our lives to God and begin to understand what matters most in life. And passion develops as we pursue what matters most.[2]

Yes, passion develops and grows as we pursue what matters most, and what matters most is knowing Christ in an authentic way. There is not a more satisfying pursuit than experiencing a rich, real, and meaningful relationship with Christ. When our hope is in Him, we will not be disappointed. God has poured His love into our hearts by His Spirit whom He has given us. He will never leave us or forsake us. He loves us with an everlasting love. He is compassionate and gracious, slow to anger and abounding in love. Oh, what joy to know Him! He redeems us, changes us, matures us, and loves us.

Paul ended his letter with a final reminder and a final greeting.

> *To our God and Father be glory forever and ever. Amen.*
> *Greet all the saints in Christ Jesus. The brothers who are with*
> *me send greetings. All the saints send you greetings, especially those*
> *who belong to Caesar's household.*[3]

Let us point our hearts upward and let our words and actions proclaim, "To our God and Father be glory forever and ever!" Yes, life is worth living, and our gifts are worth giving when we do it all for the glory of God our Father. And isn't it wonderful to call Him our *Father*. What a privilege! What a joy to be God's child and a part of His family. Paul's words sound like a family greeting between brothers and sisters. That's what we are. Let us encourage one another to go forth with outbursts of love and good deeds!

Now that you've sailed through the pages of this book, it is my sincere hope that you have come to know the essence of Paul's message to his fellow believers in Philippi. More importantly, I hope you have experienced a movement in your spirit to live and breathe your faith in Christ in a deeper and more honest way. Passionately pursuing Christ is a faith journey with a goal of not only getting to know Him better but also experiencing His power in our lives. Joy, peace, and contentment are the beautiful by-products of our walk with Him. In essence, we pursue Him because He first pursued us. May the knowledge of His abundant love for you and the strength of His Spirit give you wings to soar above the clouds of life.

> *The grace of the Lord Jesus Christ be with your spirit. Amen.*[4]

Start Your Own Positive Woman Connection and Study Questions

A Woman's Passionate Pursuit of God is part of the Positive Woman Connection Bible study series. More than five years ago, a group of women in Dallas, Texas, formed a lunchtime Bible study to encourage fellowship and feeding. Yes, I meant to say *feeding*. What I mean by that is feeding not only on a wonderful lunch but also on the rich meat of God's Word. While the ladies at our first Positive Woman Connection Bible study ate, I taught the lesson, and then they joined around their tables for a hearty discussion of what they had just learned. We want to invite you to start your own Positive Woman Connection study. You can do this in your neighborhood or at your office, church, or a local restaurant.

Who doesn't want to be a little more positive? That's why the name *Positive Woman Connection* is so inviting to women. Our intent is to connect women with one another and with the knowledge of God's Word. We encourage you to keep the study to about an hour in length so that working women as well as busy ones are able to join you. In today's fast-paced culture, we must meet people where they are. You can use this book as your guide for a twelve-week study, or you can purchase the video and discussion guide for a six-week study. You may choose to use both. Go to my website, www.PositiveLifePrinciples.com, to find out more details about how to start a study.

Study Questions

Use the following study questions, listed by chapter, for group discussion. If you are the leader, I encourage you to go to my website for free downloadable leaders' guidelines to help you lead the group discussions. Please feel free to keep in touch and let me know how your group is doing. May God bless you and lead you as you shine His light in your community.

Chapter One: Beautiful Hope from Ugly Beginnings

Kathy 1. Describe a time in your life when you experienced a rough season.

2. How did God bring good out of your personal difficulties?

3. How does praying and praising God in the middle of your challenge change the way you handle it?

4. Why is it so difficult to respond to every situation with prayer and praise?

5. Recognizing the difference Christ made in the jailer's life, tell how Christ has made a difference in your own life.

Chapter Two: Pardon My Progress

1. Tell about a time when you needed people to be patient to and understanding of you.

2. How does the attitude of thankfulness toward others change the way you interact with them? — APPRECIATION —

3. Describe what the term *affection of Christ* means to you personally.
PATIENT/FORGIVING

4. Is there someone in your life right now to whom you need to show grace and patience? What step do you need to take to "pardon their progress"? (KATHY S.— BE *PERSONAL* ROLE MODEL.)

5. What would you say is the key to having the ability to pardon people's progress? (REMEMBERING CHRIST'S GREAT SACRIFICE AND HIS UNCONDITIONAL LOVE AND GRACE TOWARD ME.)

Chapter Three: Diamonds Formed Through Difficulties

1. In what way do you need to change the way you are looking at your current challenges?

2. Who has inspired you to step forward and do something courageous?

3. What are you passionate about in life right now?

4. What step is God leading you to do to follow that passion?

5. If you were trying to encourage someone to embrace the challenges she is facing and grow from them, what would you say to her right now?

Chapter Four: Living Your Life with Passion and Purpose

1. Does passionately pursuing Christ mean that you give up everything you love?

2. How can we learn to hold onto the things of this world with a looser grip?

3. What impressed you about Amy Carmichael's story and her "Confession of Love"?

4. Have you ever had to suffer for the cause of Christ?

5. How have you experienced God's strength and perseverance through a difficulty in life?

Chapter Five: The Surprisingly Delicious Flavor of Humble Pie

1. How can an active personal prayer life help you maintain a humble heart?

2. What is one way you have recently demonstrated thoughtfulness and compassion?

3. In what way does Hudson Taylor's example inspire you to step out and care for others?

4. How does it change you to know that Jesus came as a humble servant who let go of His rights?

5. Is there a right or expectation that you need to release from your heart and mind right now?

Chapter Six: Shine Like Stars in the Universe

1. Describe the difference between working out your salvation and working for your salvation.

2. How do we become lazy in our relationship with Christ?

3. What should you do if you know what is right but don't have the desire to do what is right?

4. In what area do you tend to grumble and complain the most?

5. How does it change the way you view your circumstances when you know God has a kind intention and good purpose for you?

Chapter Seven: What Does True Devotion Look Like?

1. Who has been a spiritual encouragement to you through his or her example? *GEORGE & DAPHNE, EDITH, CONNIE HERTZLER*

2. Are you more like Timothy, Paul, or Epaphroditus? In what way?

3. How would you describe someone who is truly devoted to Christ?

4. What connection do you see between humility and being a good example to others? *BEING "APPROACHABLE"; NOT ACTING "SUPERIOR"; ADMITTING INABILITY TO BE "PERFECT" (DEPENDANCE*

5. What gifts and talents has God given you to offer in service to others? *UPON GOD?)*

Chapter Eight: Getting Rid of Garbage to Gain What Is Priceless

1. What makes us put so much value in the things we accomplish and achieve? *NEED FOR RECOGNITION/VALIDATION*

2. Why is it hard to receive a free gift?
NEED TO BE SELF-SUFFICIENT, AND NOT INDEBTED TO ANOTHER.

3. When you think about the phrase "knowing Christ and the power of His resurrection" what comes to mind? *PHYSICAL DEATH*

4. What would you say "sharing in the fellowship of His sufferings" means in real-life terms? *AS WE SUFFER (RIGHTEOUSLY), RECOGNIZE CHRIST ALSO EXPERIENCED IT SIMILARLY*

5. In what ways do you see both the power of Christ's resurrection and the fellowship of His sufferings played out in Paul's life. What about your own life?

Chapter Nine: Forget the Past and Press On to What's Ahead

1. Has there been a time in your life when you needed to mentally or physically "press on" through challenges?

2. Why does dwelling on the past tend to defeat us?

3. Why is it so easy to replay past hurts? What are some practical ways we can stop replaying the tape?

4. Reread Hebrews 12:1-2. What are some of the weights in your life that you may need to lay aside as you pursue Christ?

5. What does is it mean to you to be Christlike?

Chapter Ten: Change Your Thinking and Change Your Life

1. How do you tend to handle a situation when you see two people in conflict?

2. In what way can you apply Paul's three-part conflict resolution advice to your current relationships?

3. Is it really possible to rejoice in the Lord always? How?

4. How does fear or anxiety play a role in the conflicts you face with others?

5. How can you remind yourself to concentrate and focus on what is true and noble and right in every situation?

Chapter Eleven: The True Secret to Contentment

1. How would you describe a completely contented person?

2. How does contentment differ from complacency?

3. Why is it so difficult to be content in our society today?

4. In what area do you find it most difficult to be content?

5. Is there a time in your life when Christ gave you the strength to be content despite the circumstances?

Chapter Twelve: Be the Blessing in Your World

1. What gifts and talents has God equipped you with to be a blessing to others?

2. How are you using or planning to use those gifts?

3. What are some qualities that make a person a drain on others instead of a gift?

4. How have you seen God meet your needs through the gifts or talents of another person?

5. Describe the joy you have felt when God has used you to minister to or help others.

ℰndnotes

Introduction: Chasing Happiness and Finding Joy

1. John Blanchard, *More Gathered Gold: Treasury of Quotations for Christians* (Hertfordshire, England: Evangelical Press, 1986), 137.

2. Psalm 23:6.

Chapter One: Beautiful Hope from Ugly Beginnings

1. John Haggai, *How to Win Over Worry* (Eugene, OR: Harvest House Publishers, 2001).

2. 2 Corinthians 4:7-9.

3. Published with Mary Kenney Shave's permission."

4. 2 Corinthians 5:17.

Chapter Two: Pardon My Progress

1. 2 Corinthians 1:8-11.

2. Philippians 1:1-2.

3. Philippians 1:3-6.

4. See John 1:12 and Ephesians 1:11-14.

5. Philippians 1:7-8.

6. John 13:34-35.

7. Charles Wesley, "And Can It Be That I Should Gain?" 1738.

8. Romans 5:1-8 NLT.

9. Thelma Wells, *Don't Give In...God Wants You to Win!* (Eugene, OR: Harvest House Publishers, 2009), 39.

10. Philippians 1:9-11.

11. Luke 6:37-38.

12. 1 Corinthians 13:4-8.

Chapter Three: Diamonds Formed Through Difficulties

1. Philippians 1:12-14.

2. Walter B. Knight, "Christian Union Herald," *Knight's Master Book of New Illustrations* (Grand Rapids, MI: Eerdmans Publishing Company, 1956), 364.

3. Sinclair Ferguson, *Discovering God's Will* (Edinburgh, Scotland: Banner of Truth, 1982), 114.

4. Philippians 1:15-18.

5. Mark 9:35.

6. Mark 9:37.

7. Mark 9:38-40.

8. Hebrews 12:1-3.

Chapter Four: Living Your Life with Passion and Purpose

1. Philippians 1:20-26.

2. Psalm 103:8.

3. C. S. Lewis, *Weight of Glory* (New York, NY: HarperOne, 2001), 26.

4. Elisabeth Elliot, *A Chance to Die* (Grand Rapids, MI: Revell Publishers, 1987), 15-16.

5. Ibid., 16.

6. Ibid., 241-242.

7. *Webster's New World Dictionary, College Edition* (New York, NY: The World Publishing, 1966), 1069.

8. Luke 22:42.

9. Mark 8:33.

10. 2 Peter 1:3-4 NLT.

11. Andrew Murray, *Absolute Surrender* (Chicago, IL: Moody Publishers, 1954), 10.

12. John Blanchard, *More Gathered Gold: Treasury of Quotations for Christians* (Hertfordshire, England: Evangelical Press, 1986), 115.

13. Philippians 1:27-30.

14. Psalm 23:4 NLT.

15. James 1:2-5.

Chapter Five: The Surprisingly Delicious Flavor of Humble Pie

1. Philippians 2:1-4.

2. Psalm 34:1.

3. J. Oswald Sanders, *Spiritual Leadership* (Chicago, IL: Moody, 2007).

4. 1 Peter 5:5-7 NET.

5. Philippians 2:5-11.

6. Romans 10:9.

7. Revelation 5:11-14.

8. If you want to talk to someone personally about taking a step of faith and believing in Christ, call 1-888-Need-Him.

9. John D. Woodbridge, ed., *More than Conquerors* (Chicago, IL: Moody Press, 1992), 52.

10. Walter B. Knight, *Knight's Master Book of 4,000 Illustrations* (Grand Rapids, MI: Eerdmans Publisher, 1956), 315-316.

Chapter Six: Shine Like Stars in the Universe

1. Published with Morgan Ashbreck's permission.

2. Kevin Sherrington, "Class Acts: Competitive Spirit Gives Way to Caring After Volleyball Player's Injury," *Dallas Morning News,* November 6, 2009.

3. Philippians 2:12-13.

4. John MacArthur, *The MacArthur Bible Commentary* (Nashville, TN: Nelson Reference, 2005), 1717.

5. Ephesians 1:5 NASB.

6. Ephesians 1:9 NASB.

7. 2 Thessalonians 1:11.

8. Romans 8:28.

9. Jeremiah 29:10-11.

10. Rob Redman, "Crowded Kindness," *The High Calling of Our Daily Work* (October 27, 2002), http://www.thehighcalling.org/Library/ViewLibrary.asp?LibraryID=257.

11. Philippians 2:14-18.

12. Psalm 106:24-27 NLT.

13. James 1:19-20 NLT.

Chapter Seven: What Does True Devotion Look Like?

1. Philippians 2:19-24.

2. Acts 16:1-5.

3. 1 Timothy 4:12.

4. 2 Timothy 1:7.

5. 2 Timothy 1:3-5.

6. 1 Timothy 1:3-4.

7. Philippians 2:25-30.

8. Francis de Sales, *Introduction to the Devout Life* (Garden City, NY: Image, 1966).

9. Colossians 3:1-2.

10. Deuteronomy 6:5.

11. Matthew 22:37.

12. Published with Susie Jenning's permission. For more about Operation Care, go to www.operationcaredallas.org.

Chapter Eight: Getting Rid of Garbage to Gain What Is Priceless

1. Philippians 3:1-6.

2. Philippians 3:7-11.

3. Warren W. Wiersbe, *50 People Every Christian Should Know* (Grand Rapids, MI: Baker Books), 159-161.

4. Ephesians 5:31-32.

5. Jeremiah 9:23-24.

6. Henri J. M. Nouwen, *Clowning in Rome* (Garden City, NY: Image, 1979), 70-71.

7. John Blanchard, *More Gathered Gold: Treasury of Quotations for Christians* (Hertfordshire, England: Evangelical Press, 1986), 251.

8. Ephesians 3:16-21.

Chapter Nine: Forget the Past and Press On to What's Ahead

1. Philippians 3:12-14.

2. 1 Corinthians 9:24-27.

3. Warren W. Wiersbe, *Be Joyful* (Colorado Springs, CO: David C. Cook, 2008), 114.

4. Luke 10:41-42.

5. Psalm 27:4.

6. Colossians 3:17.

7. Colossians 3:23-24.

8. 2 Corinthians 3:18–4:1 NLT.

9. Doris Van Stone with Erwin Lutzer, *Dorie: The Girl Nobody Loved* (Chicago, IL: Moody Press, 1979), 30.

10. Joyce Vollmer Brown, *Courageous Christians* (Chicago, IL: Moody Press, 2000), 140.

11. Philippians 3:15–4:1.

12. 1 Peter 2:9-12.

Chapter Ten: Change Your Thinking and Change Your Life

1. Philippians 4:2-3.

2. Philippians 4:4-7.

3. Psalm 142:1-3 NLT.

4. Philippians 4:6-7.

5. Psalm 34:4 NLT

6. Team Hoyt, the Hoyt Foundation, "About Team Hoyt." Team Hoyt. www .TeamHoyt.com. Used with permission.

7. Philippians 4:8-9.

Chapter Eleven: The True Secret to Contentment

1. Jay MacDonald, "You Might Be a Shopaholic If…" (March 14, 2003). Bankrate .com. http://www.bankrate.com/brm/news/advice/20030314a1.asp.

2. Philippians 4:10-12.

3. 1 Timothy 6:6-8.

4. Hebrews 13:5-6.

5. NLT.

6. Philippians 4:12-13.

7. 1 Thessalonians 5:16-18.

8. James 5:16.

Chapter Twelve: Be the Blessing in Your World

1. Dr. and Mrs. William K. Henry, "Darlene Deibler Rose: A Woman of Faith." http://darlenerose.org/index.html. Used by permission.

2. Philippians 4:14-19.

3. Romans 12:1.

4. Hebrews 13:15-16.

5. Malachi 1:6-7,14.

6. Colossians 3:23-24.

7. Luke 6:38.

8. Warren W. Wiersbe, *Be Joyful* (Colorado Springs, CO: David C. Cook, 1974), 146.

9. Ephesians 3:20.

Conclusion: The Passionate Life

1. For more information about *Fresh Start,* go to www.webtv4women.tv.

2. Doug Fields, *Fresh Start: God's Invitation to a Great Life* (Nashville, TN: Thomas Nelson Publishers, 2009), 185.

3. Philippians 4:20-22.

4. Philippians 4:23.

Notes

Notes

_____

_____

_____

_____

_____

_____

_____

_____

_____

_____

_____

_____

_____

_____

_____

_____

_____

_____

_____

Notes

Notes

_____

_____

_____

_____

_____

_____

_____

_____

_____

_____

_____

_____

_____

_____

_____

_____

_____

_____

Notes

Notes

_____
_____
_____
_____
_____
_____
_____
_____
_____
_____
_____
_____
_____
_____
_____
_____
_____
_____
_____
_____
_____

Notes

_____

_____

_____

_____

_____

_____

_____

_____

_____

_____

_____

_____

_____

_____

_____

_____

_____

_____

_____

Notes

Notes

Notes

9/24/12 PG. 199 — LESSON 2, #4

PG. 53 — (TO CHECK MISSION FINANCES)

PG. 131   RE: "UNCEASING PRAYER"

CHOOSE JOY IN THE LORD
(ALWAYS) --- AND NOT IN
"CIRCUMSTANCES".

What is Stonecroft?

Connecting women with God,
each other, and their communities.

Every day Stonecroft communicates the Gospel in meaningful ways. Whether through a speaker sharing her transformational story, or side-by-side in a ministry service project, the Gospel of Jesus Christ goes forward. In one-on-one conversations with a long-term friend, and through well-developed online and print resources, the Gospel of Jesus Christ goes forward.

For nearly 75 years, we've been introducing women to Jesus Christ and training them to share His Good News with others.

Stonecroft understands and appreciates the influence of one woman's life. When you reach her, you touch everyone she knows—her family, friends, neighbors, and coworkers. The real Truth of the Gospel brings real redemption into real lives.

Our life-changing, faith-building community resources include:

- **Stonecroft Bible and Book Studies**—both topical and classic chapter-by-chapter studies. Stonecroft studies are designed for those in small groups—those who know Christ and those who do not yet know Him—to simply yet profoundly discover God's Word together

- **Small Group Studies for Christians**—these studies engage believers in God's heart for those who do not know Him. Our most recent series on evangelism includes: *Aware, Belong,* and *Call* (available in early 2012)

- **Stonecroft Life Publications**—clearly explain the Gospel through stories of people whose lives have been impacted by Jesus Christ

- **Service Activities and Events**—set the stage for women to be encouraged and equipped to hear and share the Gospel with their communities. Whether in a large venue, workshop, or small group setting, women are prepared to serve their communities with the love of Christ

- **Stonecroft Prayer**—foundational for everything we do, prayer groups, materials, and training set the focus on our reliance on God in sharing the Gospel

- **Stonecroft's Website**—stonecroft.org—offering fresh content daily to equip and encourage you.

Dedicated and enthusiastic Stonecroft staff serve you via Divisional Field Directors stationed across the United States, and a Home Office team overseeing the leadership of tens of thousands of dedicated volunteers.

Visit stonecroft.org to learn more about these and other outstanding Stonecroft resources, groups, and events.

Contact us via connections@stonecroft.org or 800.525.8627

stonecroft.org

 Karol Ladd is known as "the Positive Lady." Her heart's desire is to inspire and encourage women with a message of lasting hope and biblical truth. Karol is open, honest, and real in both her speaking and her writing. Formerly a teacher, Karol is the best-selling author of more than 25 books, including *The Power of a Positive Mom, The Power of a Positive Woman,* and *Thrive, Don't Simply Survive.* As a gifted communicator and dynamic leader, Karol is a popular speaker at women's organizations, church groups, and corporate events across the nation. Karol is a frequent guest on radio and television programs. Her most valued role is that of wife to Curt and mother to daughters Grace and Joy.

Find more information about Karol at:

> Website: www.KarolLadd.com
> Blog: www.ThriveDontSimplySurvive.Wordpress.com
> Twitter: karolladd
> Facebook: Karol Ladd

In this engaging and enlightening DVD series, bestselling author Karol Ladd shares the insight and delight of Philippians from her new book of the same title. Her humor and dynamic style shine as she leads you on a refreshing exploration of Paul's powerful message in six 30-minute sessions.

- Pardon My Progress
- Living Life with Passion
- The Delicious Flavor of Humble Pie
- Press On
- Dealing with Difficult People and Circumstances in a Positive Way
- The Key to True Contentment

With an endless supply of great stories and strong understanding of the Bible, Karol's presentation is as entertaining as it is educational. A free discussion question resource available at Karol's website will help individuals or groups embrace God's direction for their personal paths and the riches of a passionate faith.

Includes a helpful leader's guide.